DAYS OF

OR

BUCKIE & DISTRICT IN THE PAST

BY

GEO. HUTCHESON

PROVOST PUBLICATIONS
Lynnwood
8 Newlands Lane
Buckie, Banffshire
AB56 1JX

Tel: Buckie 01542 832093

Sincere thanks to the Trustees of the National
Library of Scotland for their kind permission
to reproduce the 1869 Ordnance Survey Map.

Printed by The Lossie Printers

FOREWORD

This reprint of Geo. Hutcheson's book first published in 1888 is in response to great public demand, such is the affection Days of Yore has in the hearts and minds of all who have an interest in Buckie and district, both home and away.

The foreword to the 1979 edition warned that if nothing was done to preserve our heritage it would disappear, just like a snowflake falling in a river, "A moment white - then melts forever." The warning was timely and proved a catalyst. We are happy to have been involved in the founding and development of Buckie District Fishing Heritage Society, a dedicated group of voluntary workers whose aim is to collect, preserve and make available memories, photographs and artefacts specialising in that most remarkable era in the history of 19th and 20th century Buckie, the herring boom and the hey-day of the steam drifter. Also, The Buckie Drifter, Moray Council's imaginative visitor attraction which paints the broader picture of the herring fishing and is designed to integrate with other attractions in north-east Scotland and encourage visitors to explore our area and learn about our culture.

However, we must not forget that our heritage is a continuing stream and that the post World War I evolution of the fishing industry, and the more recent, post World War II developments are equally worthy of preservation and that the younger members of the community are ideally placed to continue the story !

James Y. Merson,
Ronald S. Stewart,

20 May 1997
Buckie

Reprinted from the 1888 original by the Banffshire Advertiser for Cluny Books 1979.

Reprinted by Provost Publications 1997.

With thanks to Alan Merson for proof-reading the text.

ISBN 0 9530617 0 1

CHAPTER I

The Earliest History

*T*he earliest history of the western countries of Europe record that they were occupied by tribes who differed from each other in language, manners, and customs. When the Greek and Roman writers began to pay attention to the people to the west of them, they found Europe from the banks of the Danube to the remotest point of Ireland, peopled by a race called Gauls or Celts, or rather Kelps. Britain must have been inhabited at a period anterior to the Trojan war, since, from the statement of Herodotus, tin appears to have been exported from Britain by the Phoenician traders, and been in general use. From this we may infer that our island was then peopled by a race who had given some attention to its metallic treasures. It has been conjectured with much probability that the earliest settlers or inhabitants were of Celtic origin; but at what precise period they found their way into Britain is a question that is shrouded in the most profound obscurity. Herodian, Dio Cassius, and Tacitus refer to the Caledonian Britons as living in the most northerly part of the island and having maintained their liberty against the Romans with greater courage and unanimity than the Britons of the south, to which last characteristic allusion is made in the celebrated speech of Galgacus to his army when about to engage with the legions of Agricola. According to Tacitus this intrepid chief told his countrymen that they were the most noble among the Britons (noblissimi totius Britannia), who had never beheld slavery, far less felt it; the only difference which, from the harangue of Galgacus, seems to have then existed between the Britons of the north and those of the south. We are indebted to Julius Caesar for our first acquaintance with the history of Britain. In his day the country was possessed by upwards of forty tribes, who were not on the most friendly terms with each other.

The Bravery of the Northern Britons

North of the Firths of Forth and Clyde were the sixteen tribes which figure so conspicuously in the Roman annals. The following account of the Caledonians, and of their southern neighbours the Maeatae, is from a fragment of Dio, preserved by Xiphilin:-

"Of the (northern) Britons there are two great nations called Caledonii and Maeatae; for the rest are generally referred to these. The Maeatae dwell near that wall which divides the island into two parts. The Caledonians inhabit beyond them. They both possess rugged and dry mountains, and desert plains full of marshes. They have neither castles nor towns; nor do they cultivate the ground; but live on their flocks, and hunting, and the fruit of some trees; not eating fish though extremely plenteous. They live in tents, naked, and without buskins. Wives they have in common, and breed up their children in common. The general form of government is democratic. They are addicted to robbery, fight in cars, have small and swift horses. Their infantry are remarkable for speed in running, and for firmness in standing. Their armour consists of a shield, and a short spear, in the lower end of which is a brazen apple, whose sound, when struck, may terrify the enemy. They have also daggers. Famine, cold, and all sorts of labour they can bear, for they will even stand in their marshes, for many days, to the neck in water, and in the woods will live on the bark and roots of trees. They prepare a certain kind of food on all occasions, of which taking only a bit the size of a bean, they feel neither hunger nor thirst. Such is Britain, and such are the inhabitants of that part which wars against the Romans."

Want of Unity among the Tribes

Undoubtedly the foregoing description is a little overdone, although it is evident that the people of Caledonia were only a few stages in advance of the savage state. Their divisions into clans was the cause of much disturbance, and it was only when a foreign foe threatened them that a sense of danger forced them to unite for a time under the military authority of a Pendragon, or chief elected by common consent. The want of unity among the tribes favoured the Roman arms, Tacitus having stated that it was "rare that even two or three of them united against the common enemy," so it is not to be wondered at that Agricola managed to subjugate them as far as he found it advisable to push his conquests.

Abhorrence of Fish

It is not to be supposed that there were any fishermen in those early days since the druidical superstition proscribed the use of fish. The piscatory treasures of the rivers and waters of Caledonia were therefore but little known to the people, whose antipathy to this species of food remained in existence long after the system of the Druids had disappeared, and till the light of Christianity was diffused among them. Their entire means of subsistence were the milk and flesh of their flocks, and the produce of the chase.

Druidical Religion

Diogenes Laertius divides the tenets of the Druids into four heads:-

(1) To worship God,

(2) To abstain from evil,

(3) To exert courage,

(4) To believe in the immortality of the soul for enforcing these virtues

These tenets, if correct, must have sadly degenerated, as they are quite incompatible with the gross and revolting practices related of the Druids by more modern writers. The Druids particularly venerated the oak, believing that there was a supernatural virtue in the wood, leaves, and above all in the mistletoe. The oak woods were the most favourite places for their devotion, and the offices of their religion were always performed under heaven's broad canopy. The part appropriated for worship was enclosed in a circle, within which was placed a pillar of stone set up under an oak, and sacrifices were offered thereon.

Dio represents the Caledonians as being naked, but Herodian speaks of them as wearing a partial covering. The towns were very few, and consisted of huts covered with skins or turf. Caesar said that "what the Britons call a town is a tract of woody country, surrounded by a vallum and ditch for the security of themselves and cattle against the incursions of an enemy; for, when they have enclosed a very large circuit with felled trees, they build within it houses for themselves, and hovels for their cattle."

Notwithstanding the lightness of the attire of the ancient Caledonians in a cold and variable climate, they were very hardy and were decidedly a warlike people. The weapons they used were long broadswords, small spears, and hand daggers; and they defended their bodies in combat by a small target or shield.

The Ancient Cosmetic Art

The ancient Britons were well known to be fond of painting their bodies with a blue juice extracted from "wood called glastum, in Gaul," according to Pliny, who says that it resembled plantain. In the time of Caesar the custom was universal, the object being to present a more terrible appearance to the enemy. But fashions changed then as now, for at the end of the second or the beginning of the third century, the civilising influence of the Romans caused the application of juice to the body to be entirely discontinued in the south and a number of other barbarous practices to be given up. To distinguish those who had submitted themselves to the Roman laws from the unconquered Caledonians of the north, the Roman writers gave them the Latinized appellation of Picti, in reference to the practice of painting their bodies, which after the expedition of Severus into the north of Scotland was observed to be in general use among the various tribes. Innes, in his "Critical Essay," states that Brittannia originally signified the country of the painted or figured people.

Somewhat the same difficulties that were encountered by the English in later years in their endeavour to bring the north of Scotland into subjection was met by the Romans, as will be seen from the following account of Severus's expedition, which is taken from the fragment of Dio before referred to:-

"Of this island, not much less than half is ours. Severus, wishing to reduce the whole under his power, entered Caledonia. In his march he met with unspeakable difficulties in cutting down woods, levelling eminences, raising banks across the marshes, and building bridges over the rivers. He fought no battle, the enemy never appearing in array, but advisedly placing sheep and oxen in the way of our troops, that while our soldiers attempted to seize them, and by the fraud were drawn into defiles, they might be easily cut off. The lakes likewise were destructive to our men, as dividing them, so that they fell into ambuscades; and while they could not be brought off, were slain by our army, that they might not fall into the hands of the enemy. Owing to these causes, there died no less than 50,000 of our troops. Severus, however, did not desist till he had reached the extreme part of the island, where he diligently remarked the diversity of the solar course, and the length of the nights and days in summer and winter."

Ancient Navigation

Among such rude tribes as have been briefly described there was no commerce of any kind. Piratical excursions were not attempted, and fishing was not engaged in, so that the art of shipbuilding was unknown. At least, no memorials of shipbuilding have been found. The ancient Caledonians, however, formed canoes out of a single tree, which they hollowed by fire and propelled by means of a paddle. With these all their excursions by water were undertaken. The canoes were superseded at an early period by a craft termed "a currach." Caesar describes the currachs of South Britain as having keels and masts of the lightest wood, the hulls consisting of wicker covered over with leather. Lucan calls them little ships, in which he says the Britons were wont to navigate the ocean. Solinus says that it was common to pass between Britain and Ireland in these little ships. Adomnan, in his life of St. Columba, stated that St. Cormac sailed into the North Sea in one of these currachs, and that he remained there fourteen days in perfect safety. This vessel, however, must have been different from the currachs of Caesar, as it had all the parts of a ship with sails and oars, and was large enough to give accommodation for passengers.

Shipping

The shipping of Scotland at a comparatively recent period was inconsiderable, and even so late as 1656 comprised only 137 vessels of from 250 to 300 tons each, and aggregately 5736 tons. In 1760 the vessels employed in foreign and coasting trade and in fisheries were 999 in number, and 53,913 in tonnage. In 1828 the number of vessels belonging to Scotland was 3143, together of 300,836 tons. Aberdeen headed the list with a total of 46,587 tons; Greenock came next with 37,786 tons; then Glasgow with 36,220 tons; and Leith following with 26,107 tons. The thirteenth place was taken by Banff district with 6431 tons, Inverness taking the next place with 5092 tons. In 1835 Aberdeen had fallen to the third or fourth place, and Banff to the 15th place with 75 vessels of 4218 tons. Inverness had advanced to the 12th place with 160 vessels of 7597 tons.

The Banff, Elgin, and Nairn Tribe

In the year 81 A.D. North Britain appears to have been possessed by 21 tribes of aboriginal Britons, having little or no political connection with one another, although evidently the same people in origin and speaking the same language. The position of one of the tribes is thus defined:- "The Vacomagi inhabited the country on the southern side of the Moray Firth from the Doveran on the east to the Ness on the west, comprehending the shires of Banff, Elgin, Nairn, the eastern part of Inverness, and Braemar in Aberdeenshire. Their towns were the Ptorton of Richard, the Alata Castray of Ptolemy, at the mouth of the Varar, where the present Burghead runs into the Moray Firth; Tuessis on the eastern bank of the Spey; and Tamea and Banatia in the interior country.

The Romans in the North

In the year 140. Lollius Urbicus, the governor of the Roman provinces, and Agricola's successor, is supposed to have carried his arms as far north as the Varar or Moray Firth, and formed the whole country into a regular Roman province. The Emperor Antonius Pius extended the right of citizenship over the whole Roman empire; and thus (says Browne in the "History of the Highlands") all the inhabitants of North Britain who had resided along the east coast from the Tweed to the Moray Firth might, like St. Paul, have claimed the privileges of Roman citizens. But it is not likely that the Caledonians availed themselves of those rights. Their native pride and independence, which could not brook the idea of acknowledging any subjection to a foreign power, induced them to pay little regard to privileges which, though granted with the most praiseworthy motives, always reminded them of the causes which led to them.

Their Stations at Deskford, Bellie, Burghead and Forres

At this epoch we may date the height of the Roman power in Britain. The Romans had enlarged their territories to their greatest extent - they had conducted Iters almost to the extremities of North Britain, from the Solway and the Tyne to the Forth and Clyde, and from thence to Burghead. Browne says:-

"In proceeding from Glenmailen, the Romans directed their course northward, and crossing the Doveran, at Auchengoul, where there are still considerable remains of military works, they arrived, at the distance of thirteen statute miles, at the high ground on the north of Foggy-lone at the eastern base of the Knock-hill, the real Mons Grampius of Richard, being the first landmark seen by mariners as they approach the most easterly point of North Britain. The heights near Glenmailen afford a distinct view of the whole course of the Moray Firth, and the intermediate country through which the Romans had to pass forward to their ultimate object, Ptoroton, or Kinnaird's Head and the whole of the north-east of Buchan may be seen from the high grounds on the north of Foggy-lone.

"From the station at Knock-hill the itinerary proceeds ad Selinam of Richard, or to the rivulet Cullen, near the old tower of Deskford, at the distance of ten statute miles. This is evident from the circumstance of Roman coins found some years ago (i.e., previous to 1850) near the old bridge, a little below the tower of Deskford. Following the course of the rivulet to Inver-Cullen, and passing along the coast of the Moray Firth, the Roman armies arrived at the Roman post which is still to be seen on the high bank of the Spey, the Tuessis of Ptolemy and Richard, below the church of Bellie, a distance of nineteen statute miles.

About half a mile north-east of the ruins of Bellie, on a bank overlooking the low fluviated ground of the river, are the remains of a Roman encampment. It is situated upon a flat surface, and forms nearly a rectangular parallelogram of 888 feet by 333; but the west side, and the greater part of the north end of the parallelogram are now wanting. It is singular that the ford on the Spey, by which the Romans were enabled to connect their stations in the north, during the second century, should have facilitated the passage of the Duke of Cumberland in April, 1746, when he pressed forward 'in order to decide,' says Chalmers, 'the fate of the Gaelic descendants of the ancient race.'

"From their station on the eastern bank of the Spey, with the Moray Firth close to their right, they were only one day's march from the Alatta-Castray of Ptolemy, the Ptoroton of Richard, the Burgh-head of modern geographers, at the mouth of the Estuary of Varar. The north and west sides of the promontory called Burgh-head are steep rocks washed by the sea, and which rises 60 feet above the level of the low-water mark; the area on the top of the head is 300 feet long on the east side, and 520 feet long on the west side; it is 260 feet broad, and contains rather more than two English acres. A strong rampart twenty feet high, built with old planks, cased with stone and lime, appears to have surrounded it; the south and east sides are pretty entire, but the north and west sides are much demolished. On the east side of this height, and about 40 feet below the summit, there is an area 650 feet long, and 150 feet wide, containing upwards of three English acres. The space occupied by the ruins of the ramparts which have fallen down, is not included in this measurement. It appears to have been surrounded with a very strong rampart of stone which is now much demolished. On the south and land side of these fortified areas, two deep ditches are carried across the neck of this promontory; these ditches were, in 1792, when surveyed by Chapman, from sixteen to twenty feet deep, from twelve to sixteen feet wide at the bottom, and from forty to fifty feet wide at the top. The bottoms of the ditches were then 25 feet above the level of the sea at high water, and are considerably higher than the extensive tract of flat ground on the land side. The ditches, ramparts, rocks, and waste ground, which surrounded the areas above described, contain upwards of five English acres.

"As the Romans had other stations in the north besides those noticed, they did not always in returning to the south follow the course of the Iter just described. They had another Iter, the first station of which from the Burgh-head was the Varis of Richard, now Forres, a distance of eight statute miles. It is singular that the Gaelic name of Forres is Faris, which corresponds so exactly with Varis as to make it certain that Forres and Varis of Richard are the same. Besides, when the streets of Forres were dug up in order to repair the pavement, there were discovered several Roman coins, and a Roman medallion in soft metal, which resembled a mixture of lead and tin."

It may be said that within the limits of the ancient fort at Burghead a Roman bath was discovered, as also a stone on which there was the drawing of a bull, evidently also the work of Roman hands.

In the year 170 the Romans abandoned North Britain without molestation, but the tribes pillaging the country in 209 Severus marched northwards with an immense army, 50,000 of whom fell prey to the attacks of the Caledonians and the severity of the weather.

A Mutinous Chieftain

In the year 881 Aodh or Hugh succeeded to the throne of Scotland, but his reign was short and troublesome. Grig, an artful chieftain, who was Maormor of the country between the Dee and the Spey, raised a revolt. Aodh endeavoured to put it down, but did not succeed. He was wounded in the bloody field of Strathallan, and was carried to

Inverurie, where he died after lingering two months, having only held the sceptre for one year. Grig then assumed the crown, and associated with him Eoacha, the British king of Strathclyde. After a reign of eleven years both were forced to abdicate.

The Battle of the Bauds

The country about this time began to be infested by the piratical excursions of the Danes. Tradition has it that the creek at Portknockie was a favourite landing place of these marauders, and history mentions that a battle was fought in 961 on the moor near Portknockie. The encounter was a very severe one, and it is known as the battle of the Bauds. It resulted in the complete overthrow of the Danes, but the Scotch king, Indulph, lost his life. During the eight years of his reign he had had many encounters with these pirates. His grave is said to be on an eminence near Woodside, and was covered over with stones, the place being known as the King's cairn. Not far distant are a great number of small cairns, alleged to be the burial-places of the Danes who fell in the engagement. An ancient grave which was found on the moor of Portknockie has also been thought by some to have been the last resting place of Indulph. (Carruthers says that Indulph accidently fell in with a fresh party of Danes in "the glen" after routing the main body, and that he received a deadly wound in the head. Further, that Indulph was carried to Cullen, where he died, and his body afterwards conveyed across country and buried. Up to the beginning of this century there were a number of cairns on the Bauds.) The exact site of the battle is said to lie alongside the Fochabers and Cullen turnpike road on the second croft occupied by Mr Wiseman, east of the road that leads down to Findochty. A good many of the invaders found graves between Smithstown and Hillhead of Findochty, towards the sea, as if killed while retreating towards the shore for the purpose of escaping, numerous tumuli or grave mounds having been found. A relic of the bloody affray is in the hands of Mrs Stephen, Milton of Deskford, in the shape of a stone-axe of well-finished proportions.

A Portknockie Tradition

A curious tradition regarding the Danes may be narrated. On one of their piratical incursions they succeeded in establishing themselves at Portknockie to the intense disgust of the ancient inhabitants of the district. In the woods above Portknockie the Scotch eagerly consulted as to how they were to drive the invaders from the shore. The result of the consultation was that they cut down trees, and carrying them so that their persons should not be seen from the front, they moved down towards Portknockie. The pirates gazed with horror at what appeared to be a forest of trees advancing upon them, and fled in greatest consternation to their vessels, while many jumped into the sea at the Scarnose and were drowned.

Aberdeenshire Tradition

Another tradition may be given, although it does not concern this immediate district. The Danes, it is said, on one occasion secured a footing at Cruden, some miles from Peterhead, and many women were taken captive, perhaps willingly. The victors celebrated their victory by a drunken carousal in the evening, and sought to woo the embraces of their fair prisoners. But, according to instructions, as opportunity offered, the women plunged a knife or dagger into the hearts of their would-be lovers, exclaiming at the same time, "Hallo! een!" and lighting a torch which was kept ignited for a few seconds. The fathers, husbands, and brothers of the women, grasping their weapons with deadly import, were meantime peering from adjoining places of shelter at the strange scene, lit up by the camp fires, and watching for the torch signal and listening for the cry that signified the death of a Dane. When it appeared that a sufficient number of the invaders had been killed to ensure a likelihood of success to the Scotch over the survivors, they burst upon the enemy and exacted ample vengeance. Cruden, it is said, thus obtained its name from the victory, or the "crowing over the Danes," and the night has since been known as "Hallow E'en."

The Danes at Speymouth

Malcolm II. ascended the throne in 1003. The Danes at the time had obtained a firm footing in England, and directed their attention in an especial manner to Scotland, which they were in the hopes of subduing. They had hitherto been defeated in every attempt they had made to establish themselves in the north, but having become powerful by their vast possessions in England they considered that they now had great chances of success in their favour. Accordingly, immense preparations were made by the celebrated Sweyn to invade Scotland. Powerful armies were raised in Norway and Denmark, and a suitable fleet equipped. Sigurd, the Earl of Orkney, carried on a harassing and predatory warfare on the shores of the Moray Firth, which he continued even after a matrimonial alliance with Malcolm, whose daughter he married; but this was no singular trait in the character of a viking, who plundered friends and foes. The scene of Sigurd's operations was chosen by his brother northmen for making a descent, which they effected near Speymouth.

Murder of Nairn Garrison

They carried fire and sword through Moray and laid siege to the fortress of Nairne, one of the strongest in the north. Malcolm encamped near Kilfloss, or Kinloss, and after a severe action was forced to retreat severely wounded. Nairne then surrendered, when there seemed no chance of assistance being obtained, and the whole garrison were hanged notwithstanding a capitulation which stipulated for their lives and properties.

In the ensuing spring Malcolm defeated the Danes at Mortlach after a very fierce conflict. In gratitude to God for his victory he endowed a religious house near the scene of the action. Pope Benedict confirmed the endowment, and Mortlach soon became the residence of a bishop.

A battle afterwards took place at Cruden between Malcolm and Canute, in which the Danes had a great many slain. After the battle a stipulation was made by which the Danes agreed to evacuate the Burgh-head of Moray, and finally to leave every part of the kingdom, which they accordingly did in 1014, the Danes having apparently established themselves at the Roman fort of Burghead.

Supposed evidence of the Danes at Buckie

There is every reason to suppose that many of the Danes were slain in the vicinity of Buckie, but history is silent on the matter. East of the Cluny Harbour, where fish-houses, sawmills, etc., now are, was from 50 to 80 years ago a wilderness of sandy hillocks, and was known as the Links. There was no regularly-formed road to the east, carts and pedestrians taking the route that was handiest, which meant a winding course round the sand hillocks. The Links, as may be supposed, were a favourite place with the youth of Buckie, and here the young folk often came to amuse themselves. The undermining of banks by sand being taken away, and their demolition by boys of an inquisitive nature, frequently brought to view great quantities of bones, which were supposed to be those of Danes who had perished at the place. There are several old men in Buckie who used to indulge in football, the ball being a skull, and the game was none the less heartily engaged in because it was thought that the ball had once been the head of one of our ancient enemies the Danes.

CHAPTER II
The Gordons

A name frequently to be met with in Scottish history is that of Gordon. The Gordons are supposed to have come from France into Scotland about the time of William the Conqueror. An old MS. by John Gordon, son of George Gordon of Prony, states that the first Gordon who got the lands of Long Gordon from Malcolm III. was named Sir Adam Gordon, and that he died valiantly fighting at the siege of Alnwick. One Adam Gordon lived at the time of Robert the Bruce, and at first sided with Baliol. Finding that Baliol was endeavouring to bring his native country under the servitude of a foreign nation, he, however, changed his allegiance to Bruce. Gordon received the order of knighthood from King Robert, and assisted to defeat the Cummings near Inverurie, in recompense for which he received the large and fertile lordship of Strathbogie. About the year 1358 King David bestowed on a Sir John Gordon the lands and forests of Enzie and Boyne, which were confirmed to the first Earl of Huntly, his descendant, in a charter dated March 15, 1457.

A "Letterfourie" Admiral

Abercromby says that King James the 4th had a fleet of ships in the river Forth, and among many others of which it was composed, the Michael, Margaret, and James were universally admired for their bulk and strength. He gave the command of the whole to Sir James Gordon of Letterfury (? Letterfourie), brother to the Earl of Huntly, of whose valour and fidelity he was sufficiently assured, with letters of mark, and orders to transport the Earl of Arran and 3000 or 4000 men under his conduct to France whom to encourage the more the King in person goes aboard the Michael and accompanies them to the Island of May.

The Legitimacy of a Laird of Buckie

In "The history of the Illustrious Family of Gordon" is the following:- "Ferrerius says that Elizabeth Gordon (mother of the first Earl of Huntly), heiress of Huntly had two natural brothers born to her father by Elizabeth Cruickshank, daughter to Cruickshanks of Assuanly, the eldest called John of Scurdarg, of whom are descended many gentlemen of considerable estates; and the Laird of Pitlurg has been, by the descendants of his family, esteemed the representative of him. The Laird of Buckie, and those of his family, pretend to the same; but neither of them have ancient writs to make good their claims, and so I shall not take it on me to determine in it, but briefly hint at what both of them advance for themselves. Buckie says that John of Scurdarg, his predecessor, was first married to the daughter of Macleod of Heris, by whom he had one son called Gordon of Enzie of whom this Laird of Buckie is descended. On the other side, Pitlurg, and those of his family say that John was not married to that lady, but only hand-fasted to her; and that he married Maitland of Gight's daughter, by whom he had John Gordon of Botery, the Laird of Straloch's predecessor. It would seem that the late Duke of Gordon looked upon Pitlurg's predecessor as the eldest of John's sons; for in a tailzie or destination he made of his estate, of the date at Edinburgh, February 25, 1707, in the substitution he prefers Pitlurg to Buckie. But neither of these gentlemen having now any old writs to decide this controversy, I shall not take upon me to determine anything about it, but leave the same as I found it. However, both these ancient families afforded many brave gentlemen, who upon all occasions valiantly ventured their lives with their chief in the defence of their king and country."

A Quarrel between the Gordons and Ogilvies

In the summer of 1562 Sir John Gordon, the third son of the Earl of Huntly, and Lord Ogilvie, between whom there was a dispute as to some property, in Banffshire no doubt, met in the streets of Edinburgh, and being both attended by armed followers a scuffle ensued in which Lord Ogilvie was dangerously wounded. Both of the offenders were apprehended by magistrates, and Queen Mary gave orders that they should be confined. The friends of each party began to convene their vassals and dependents in order to overawe, or frustrate the decisions of justice. Gordon, however, effected his escape.

Queen Mary in the North

The Queen being in the north, Lady Huntly interceeded for pardon for Sir John Gordon, but her Majesty peremptorily required that he should again deliver himself into the hands of justice and rely on her clemency. Gordon was persuaded to do so; and being enjoined by the Queen to enter himself prisoner in the Castle of Stirling, the governor of which was Lord Erskine, the Earl of Mar's uncle, he promised likewise to obey that command. The Queen's severity and the place in which she appointed Gordon to be confined, were interpreted to be marks of the Earl of Mar's influence, there being the greatest jealousy on the part of Huntly against Mar and other ministers of the day. Gordon set out towards Stirling, but escaped and returned to take command of his followers, who were rising in arms all over the north. History now becomes very conflicting. Buchanan and Robertson say that Huntly had a scheme devised for the murder of Mar, Morton, and Maitland, but on the other hand this is denied. On the arrival of Queen Mary at Inverness she was refused admission to the castle - by Huntly's orders it is said and contradicted - and was obliged to lodge in the town, which was quickly surrounded by a multitude of the Earl's followers. To secure her escape "ships were ordered into the river, but by the loyalty of the Monroes, Frasers, Mackintoshes, and other clans," she was saved from danger, being only attended by a small retinue of her own. The castle was also taken and the governor executed. Afterwards Lord Erskine was made Earl of Moray, with the estate annexed to that dignity, which, says Crawford, had been in the possession of the Earl of Huntly since the year 1548. Huntly then broke into open rebellion, and a battle was fought at Corrichie, in Aberdeenshire, while the Queen was returning South. Huntly was trodden under foot by his retreating party, and his two sons, Sir John and Adam, were captured and taken to Aberdeen. Both were sentenced to be beheaded, but the latter had the punishment remitted on account of his youth. The author of "The History of the Illustrious Family of Gordon" says Murray forced the Queen to witness the execution of Sir John Gordon, and that Mary shed tears at the death of one who had aspired to the honour of being her husband. The incidents connected with the visit of Queen Mary to the north, it may be said, are the most intricate and mysterious passages in Scottish history.

Death of a John Gordon of Buckie

Towards the close of the year 1571 or the beginning of 1572, a battle was fought at Tulliangus, not far from Castle Forbes, between the Forbeses and the Gordons, in which 100 of the former were killed. Of the latter the only person of note who was killed was John Gordon of Buckie.

Rebellion against the Earl of Huntly

The Earl of Huntly was a great favourite with James the 6th, but finding himself in danger from the prevailing faction he retired to his possessions in the north for the purpose of improving his estate and enjoying domestic quiet. One of his first measures was to erect a castle at Ruthven in Badenoch. This gave great offence to Mackintosh, the chief of the Clan Chattan, and his people, as they considered that the object of its erection was to overawe the clan. Being the Earl's vassals and tenants they were bound to certain services, among which the furnishing of building materials formed a chief part; but this obligation they refused to fulfil. Matters culminated in the murder of a servant of the brother of Sir Thomas Gordon of Cluny by John Grant, the tutor of Ballendalloch. Grant not being delivered up, the Earl of Huntly proclaimed his disobedient vassals rebels, and obtained a royal commission in 1590 to invade and apprehend them. To consult on the best means of defending themselves the Earls of Moray and Athole, the Dunbars, the Clan Chattan, the Grants, and the Laird of Cadell, and others of their party, met at Forres. On the one hand Mackintosh, Grant, and Cadell, advised the Earls to immediately collect their forces and oppose Huntly; but the Dunbars, on the other hand, held that they were not in a fit condition to make a successful stand against their formidable opponents. In the midst of these deliberations Huntly suddenly made his appearance in the neighbourhood of Forres, and the whole party, with the exception of the Earl of Moray, left the town in hot haste. The fugitives fled to Tarnoway, where they were followed by Huntly. While John Gordon, brother of Cluny, was reconnoitring he was shot dead. The castle being well protected Huntly returned home, and afterwards went to Edinburgh.

The Earl of Moray slain

Shortly after his arrival the Earl of Bothwell made an attack upon Holyrood with the view of seizing Chancellor Maitland, but failing in his object he had to flee to the north to escape the vengeance of the King. The Earl of Huntly and the Duke of Lennox were commissioned to capture him, and found that he was being harboured by the Earl of Moray at Dunibristle. A party was then collected, and on reaching Dunibristle, the Earl of Huntly sent Captain John Gordon, brother of Gordon of Gight, with a summons desiring the Earl of Moray to surrender himself a a prisoner. The reply was a shot which severely wounded the bearer of the despatch. Huntly then entered the house by force, giving orders that the Earl of Moray was to be taken alive if possible. Sir Thomas Gordon, recollecting the fate of his brother at Tarnoway, and Gordon of Gight, who saw his brother lying wounded before his eyes, entirely disregarded the injunction, and seeing the Earl endeavouring to escape by the rocks at the seashore, followed him and slew him.

John Gordon of Buckie as a Mediator

The Earl of Huntly immediately despatched John Gordon of Buckie to Edinburgh to lay statement before the King and the Chancellor; but the Earl of Moray having been one of the heads of the Protestant party the matter took a religious turn, and Huntly was denounced as a murderer who wished to advance the interests of the Romish Church by imbruing his hands in the blood of his Protestant countrymen. The tumult was such that the King was obliged to cancel the commission he had given to the Earl of Huntly, and Captain John Gordon who had been left at Inverkeithing for the recovery of his wounds was taken prisoner by the Earl of Moray's friends and carried to Edinburgh. Here he was tried before a jury, and contrary to law and justice, was condemned and executed for having assisted the Earl of Huntly while acting under a royal commission. This circumstance caused John Gordon of Buckie, who was master of the King's household, to flee from Edinburgh, and he narrowly escaped with his life. The Earl of Huntly was called upon to stand trial, and was committed a prisoner to the Castle of Blackness but was released by the King in the course of eight days. The foregoing, it may be said, is about the earliest references to be found regarding the name "Buckie."

A Banff Counterfeiter

During the year 1612 a man named Arthur Smith, who resided in Banff and counterfeited coin of the realm, fled to Sutherland, where he was apprehended for passing base coin and imprisoned in Edinburgh for trial. An accomplice was burned at the stake. During Smith's imprisonment he constructed a lock of ingenious device which was presented to the King, who was so delighted with it that he finally liberated him. Smith afterwards went to Caithness, and was taken into the employ of the Earl of Caithness, who resided at Castle Sinclair. A great inundation of counterfeit coin taking place, Sir Robert Gordon and his nephew, Donald Mackay, were empowered by the King and Privy Council to apprehend Smith. Mackay succeeded in capturing Smith, and to prevent him being retaken by a tumultuous mob in Thurso he was killed. A combat took place in which a number on both sides were killed. On the Earl of Caithness hearing of the affair he resolved to prosecute Donald Mackay. Both parties appeared at Edinburgh, each attended by a large company, among the friends of Sir Robert Gordon and Mackay being Buckie "and other gentlemen of respectability." On the suggestion of the Privy Council the matter was remitted to the arbitration of mutual friends, which brought a squabble to a close that had created great uproar and discord in the north of Scotland.

Dispute between the Earl of Enzie and Mackintosh

George, Lord Gordon, eldest son of the first Marquis of Huntly, was termed the Earl of Enzie. A dispute arose in 1618 between the Earl and the Clan Chattan in regard to the tithes of Culloden, to which the Earl of Enzie had a claim. The Earl asked the assistance of Sir Robert Gordon, the Earl of Sutherland's tutor, who left Sutherland for the Bog o' Gight (now Gordon Castle), where the Marquis of Huntly and the Earl then were. In passing, Sir Robert called on Macintosh at Culloden with the view of effecting a compromise, but without result. The Earl of Enzie then proceeded to Culloden with 1100 horsemen, and 600 Highlanders on foot, Macintosh having collected the clans of Chattan, Grant, and Kenzie for the purpose of resistance; but at the solicitation of Lord Lovat he sent the keys of the castle to the Earl of Enzie, and the dispute was accordingly settled in a most harmonious manner.

Frendraught and Rothiemay quarrel

In 1629 a dispute arose between James Crighton of Frendret, or Frendraught, and William Gordon of Rothiemay, which ended in tragic consequences. These two gentlemen were near neighbours, and their lands lay adjacent to each other. Part of Gordon's lands, which marched those of Crighton's, were purchased by the latter, but an irreconcilable dispute occurred about the right to the salmon fishings belonging to these lands. The parties took the matter to law, and Crighton succeeded in getting Gordon denounced rebel. He had previously treated Rothiemay very harshly, and the latter, stung by the severity of his opponent, would not listen to the peaceful advice of his best friends. Determined to set the law at defiance he collected a number of loose and disorderly characters and annoyed Frendraught, who appealed to the Privy Council and obtained a commission to apprehend Rothiemay and his associates. In the execution of this task he was assisted by Sir George Ogilvie of Banff and other gentlemen. On the 1st of January, 1630, Crighton proceeded to Rothiemay with a resolution either to apprehend Gordon, or set him at defiance by affronting him. He was incited the more to follow this course, as young Rothiemay, at the head of a party, had come a short time before to the very doors of Frendraught, and insulted him to his face. When Rothiemay heard of Frendraught's advance he left his house, accompanied by his eldest son, John Gordon, and a considerable party, and crossing the

Deveron went forward to meet Frendraught. A sharp conflict ensued in which Frendraught was successful, and Rothiemay left on the field covered with wounds. The son of the deceased laird determined to avenge his father's death, and associated with James Grant and other freebooters for the purpose of laying waste Frendraught's lands. Frendraught appealed to the King, and the Privy Council granted a commission to Frendraught and others to apprehend John Gordon and his associates. A warrant was also given to the same effect to Sir Robert Gordon and Sir William Seaton of Killesmuir, the Earl of Moray (the King's lieutenant in the north, having failed to quell the disturbances), with instructions to obtain the aid of the Marquis of Huntly. By Sir Robert's aid the matter was finally amicably arranged, Frendraught willingly paying fifty thousand merks to the wife of the late Laird of Rothiemay in compensation for the loss of her husband.

Frendraught and Pitcaple

The Laird of Frendraught had scarcely reconciled himself with Rothiemay when he got into another dispute with the Laird of Pitcaple, who was named James Meldrum. Meldrum had assisted Frendraught in his forays against Rothiemay, and considered that he had not been amply recompensed for his services. In revenge, he privately carried away two horses during the night from Frendraught's park. Meldrum was thereupon prosecuted for theft, but as he did not appear he was declared a rebel, and Frendraught was commissioned to apprehend him. Meldrum then took refuge with John Leslie of Pitcaple, his brother-in-law. Frendraught proceeded to Pitcaple's lands, where he met James Leslie, the second son of the Laird of Pitcaple. An argument took place, when Robert Crighton of Couland, a kinsman of Frendraught, drew a pistol from his belt and shot Leslie in the arm, who was thereupon carried home apparently in a dying state. The Leslies then took up arms against Frendraught, who went to the Marquis of Huntly and the Earl of Moray to express his regret at the affair, and to ask their kindly interference to bring matters to an amicable settlement. The Marquis sent for Pitcaple to come to the Bog of Gight to confer with him; but, before setting out, he mounted and equipped thirty horsemen in consequence of information he had received that Fredraught was at the Bog. At the meeting with the Marquis, Pitcaple complained heavily of the injury his son had sustained, and hotly said that he would revenge himself before he returned home. The Marquis insisted that Frendraught had done him no wrong, and endeavoured to dissuade him from putting his threat into execution; but Pitcaple was so displeased at the Marquis for thus expressing himself that he suddenly mounted his horse and set off, leaving Frendraught behind him. The Marquis of Huntly, afraid of the consequences, detained Frendraught two days with him in the Bog of Gight, and, hearing that the Leslies had assembled and lay in wait for Frendraught, watching his return home, the Marquis sent his son John, Viscount of Aboyne, and the Laird of Rothiemay along with him to protect and defend him if necessary. They arrived at Frendraught without interruption, and agreed to remain there all night.

A Disastrous Fire

The sleeping apartment of the Viscount was in the old tower of Frendraught, leading off from the hall. Immediately below this apartment was a vault, in the bottom of which was a round hole of considerable depth. Robert Gordon, a servant of the Viscount, and his page, English Will, as he was called, also slept in the same chamber. The Laird of Rothiemay, with some servants, were put into an upper chamber immediately above that in which the Viscount slept; and in another apartment, directly over the latter were George Chalmer of Noth, Captain Rollock, one of Frendraught's party, and George Gordon, another of the Viscount's servants. After midnight the whole of the tower almost simultaneously took fire, and so suddenly and furiously did the flames consume the edifice that the Viscount, the Laird of Rothiemay, English Will, Colonel Ivat, one of Aboyne's friends, and two other persons, perished in the flames. Lord Aboyne might have saved himself as did others, but instead of endeavouring immediately to escape he ran upstairs for the purpose of awakening Rothiemay. While so engaged the staircase and ceiling of Rothiemay's apartment took fire, and, being prevented from descending by the flames which filled the staircase, they ran from window to window of the apartment piteously and unavailingly calling for help. The news of this calamitous event spread speedily throughout the kingdom, and the fate of the unfortunate sufferers was deeply deplored. How the fire originated was never known, but it was proved that the Leslies had threatened to burn the house of Frendraught, a negotiation having been entered into to that effect with James Grant, the rebel, who, along with John Meldrum and Alexander Leslie, were apprehended. The Bishops of Aberdeen and Moray, Lord Carnegie, and Crowner Bruce were appointed by the Privy Council to investigate the circumstances which led to the fire. They accordingly went to Frendraught, where they were met by Lords Gordon, Ogilvie, and Deskford. Their decision was that the fire must have been caused by some engine from without, or must have been raised intentionally within the vaults or chambers of the tower. Meldrum was tried at Edinburgh, and on the evidence of Sir George Ogilvie, Laird of Banff, and George Baird, bailie of Banff, he was condemned, and was accordingly hanged and quartered at the cross of Edinburgh. Grant, on the other hand, managed to escape.

Letterfourie Imprisoned and Liberated

Frendraught's enemies, after the execution of Meldrum, did not abate their persecution, his cattle being carried off, and his tenants expelled. The heads of the families whose sons had joined the marauders in pillaging Frendraught's lands were summoned to Edinburgh, When Letterfourie, Park, Tilliangus, Terrisoule, Invermarkie, Tulloch, Ardlogy, and several other persons of the surname Gordon, were committed to prison, but shortly afterwards released, and the Marquis of Huntly obliged to find caution for them. The Marquis thereupon apprehended twelve of the pillagers who were sent to Edinburgh and several of them executed. Sir Adam Gordon of the Park, finding it likely that he would be apprehended, charged James Gordon of Letterfourie with having employed him and his associates, in the name of the Marquis, against the Laird of Frendraught. Letterfourie was accordingly cited to appear at Edinburgh for trial, and on being confronted with Adam Gordon denied everything, but was committed a close prisoner to jail. The Marquis appeared at Edinburgh on the 15th January, 1638, and was "upon presumption" likewise committed to prison. There being no proof against the two, however, they were discharged by command of the King. On the 13th day of June of the same year the Marquis died at Dundee and was interred in the family vault at Elgin, having been a most remarkable man, well entitled to veneration and esteem for his love of justice and general kindliness of disposition.

CHAPTER III

The Start of Fishing Stations

*T*he growth of Buckie is undoubtedly due to the fisheries. The oldest station in the parish is Nether Buckie, which has been connected with fishing for very close on two and a half centuries. Porteasy or Portessie became a fishing station in 1727, when five houses were built by the proprietor of Rannas for the accommodation of the original fishermen, who came from Findhorn. A small thatched building on the west side of the village is pointed out as the first house in Portessie. At this time Buckie had 5 boats, Findochty 3, and Portknockie 5. Findochty was settled in 1716 by fishers from Fraserburgh, who made a start with 3 boats. The first house in Portknockie is said to have been built in 1677, the first settlers having come from the neighbouring town of Old Cullen, which stood where Seafield or Cullen House, the seat of the Earls of Findlater or Seafield, now stands. The following anecdote, taken from the old "Statistical Account," tells the story of the origin of Portknockie as a fishing station:- "About twenty years ago died Katie Slater, aged ninety-six. Like many old people, she was unable to tell her age precisely, but she recollects she was as old as the House of Farskane, as her father had often told that he built the first house in Portknockie the same year in which the House of Farskane was built, and that she was brought from Cullen to it, and rocked in a fisher's scull instead of a cradle. From the date on the old House of Farskane, it appears to have been built in 1677."

A Few of the Earliest Fishers

A hundred years ago nearly the whole of the residenters in the Seatown of Buckie were called Cowie or Murray. The latter, it is said, came from Helmsdale; the Fletts of Findochty came from Shetland on the invitation of John Ord, the Laird of Findochty; the Clarks, Farquhars, and Gardens of Portessie were originally farmers in the district, but took to fishing at the beginning of this century; and a farm servant called Imlach also settled at Portessie as a fisherman. Two of the original settlers at Portessie were families of the name of Smith - one came from Findhorn, and the other from Maviestown, between Findhorn and Nairn. Two Sclaters came from Orkney and settled in the district about 160 years ago. It appears that two brothers of that name were in the habit of paying periodical visits to the district for the purpose of disposing of butter, cheese and worsted goods and other luxuries. They were dressed in suits of home-spun cloth, and taking a fancy to Banffshire the one took up his abode permanently at Portknockie, and the other settled in Buckie.

The Herring Fishing

In 1793 we find that in Nether Buckie there were 102 houses with 400 inhabitants; and in Easter Buckie there were 63 houses with 303 inhabitants. The proprietor of the former place was Mr Dunbar, and the latter belonged to Mr Baron Gordon. In the year mentioned there were 14 boats and one yawl employed in the fisheries. The former were of 9 tons each, and the latter of 4 tons. Three of the boats and the yawl belonged to the Duke of Gordon, 3 boats belonged to Mr Dunbar, and the remaining 8 to Mr Baron Gordon. In 1793 Portessie had 44 houses, 178 inhabitants, and 5 large and 7 small boats; Findochty comprised 45 houses, 162 inhabitants, and 4 large and 6 small boats; and Portknockie had 80 houses, 243 inhabitants, and 7 large and 9 small boats. The large boats in the three villages last mentioned were about 10 tons each, and the small ones 4 tons each. The original cost of one of the former, including sails, oars, and lines was about £24; the small boats cost half that sum. The proprietors allowed £11 to every crew purchasing a new boat, which was understood to last for seven years, and in return a yearly rent was paid for the craft of £5 3s 3d, and 6 dried cod or ling. The small boats were the property of the fishermen, but none of them existing at Buckie the large boats had to be used at all seasons. The lesser boats were used from the end of February to the end of July, and the large ones at other times. The latter were manned by a crew of six men and a boy, and each man was understood to have a line with a 100 to 120 hooks upon it; and the boy carried a line half the length of a man's. From the beginning of May the boats went off as far as 23 leagues. In the Skate Hole ling and skate were found most plentifully. About the end of June the dried fish were taken in the boats to towns in the Moray Firth, and there sold. The value of the fish each large boat took away for sale was generally from £60 to £70. The small boats had a crew of five men and a boy. Herrings were sometimes found very plentifully on the coast. The herring fishing was prosecuted for six weeks from 24th July, during which time the income of the fishermen was often as large as during the other 46 weeks of the year. During the herring fishing the boats were manned by 4 men, who had each at least four nets, which cost him £4. The average take landed by a boat during the season was from 50 to 100 barrels, for which 10s per barrel on an average and a bottle of whisky was paid. In 1786 so many herrings were caught that great quantities of them had to be thrown into the bay. This seemed to have a depressing effect on the herring fishing, so that it was not prosecuted again until 1791 and 1792, when some boats were employed by J. Geddes & Son. In 1792 a new departure was made in the fishing industry, all the fishermen being engaged by Selbey & Co., London, or with the Northumberland Fishery Company, to fish for lobsters which were paid for at the rate of 2 1/2d each. The fishermen were all supplied with sciffs for this purpose.

Losses at Sea

From 1723 to 1793 Buckie lost 8 boats with crews and passengers amounting to 60 men and boys. During that period as many people in the town had not died a natural death. Portessie lost 4 men. In 1755 Findochty lost 1 boat and 7 men. Within 25 years of last century Portknockie lost 5 boats and 3 crews, and 2 yawls and 6 men and boys, giving a total loss of 41 men and boys. About 140 years ago a small fishing community resided a small distance up the Burn of Freuchny. They comprised a complete crew, but about 1750 the boat was lost at sea and the whole of the men were drowned. In a short time the small village of Freuchny became extinct, one of the widows, a Mrs Thomson, removing to the Seatown of Buckie.

A number of very serious disasters occurred about the beginning of this century. On New Christmas, 1806, a Portessie boat was lost with all hands. This was the day on which the village of Stotfield lost four crews, the only males left in the village being a few children, a boy of 14 years of age, and an old publican who had not been in the habit of going to sea for several years. The latter, George Garden, got a boat built, and induced his brother to leave Portessie and go to Stotfield. The two men then took the oldest boys to sea with them, and taught them the industry at which their fathers had lost their lives, thus doubtless preserving Stotfield from extinction as a fishing village.

From the old minutes of Presbytery, which have been published by Mr Crammond, M.A., Cullen, whose researches are of a particularly valuable nature, and are characterised by a completeness and harmony in arrangement that does him the greatest credit, we find that in 1756 a collection was ordered for some widows and families at Findochtie, whose husbands and heads had been lately lost at sea.

On April 5th, 1765, "a fishing boat belonging to the parish of Rathven was cast away in a violent storm, and all the men, 7 in number, were drowned. Six families were left destitute." Collections in this case were also made.

In 1780 the following minute was made:- "Collections ordered for 6 widows and 18 children, in Rathven, whose husbands and parents perished at sea, 9th March."

"1787.- Collections ordered for the widows and children of 35 fishermen belonging to Buckie and Portknocky who perished at sea."

"1819.- Collected £4 9s 3d for the families of seamen belonging to the parish of Rathven who perished in March last."

"1821.- Collected £5 13s for the families of the seamen of Portknockie."

At the beginning of this century there were 11 boats belonging to Easter Buckie, and latterly the number was increased to 12. This number, however, was considered very unlucky by the fishermen of those days, and is still so considered by more than fishermen. In the year 1818 a boat was lost with 6 hands, which was held to be an omen as to the unluckiness of having 12 boats. For a few years the number remained at 11, and then gradually increased. At this time there were 8 boats belonging to Nether Buckie, and an addition of one taking place a disaster brought the number of boats again down to 8.

"The Joogs"

In addition to paying the laird so much money and a certain quantity of fish (or their value), in return for being provided with boats, the fishermen were compelled to give "binnage freights," or, in other words, had to place themselves and boats at the disposal of the laird for the purpose of conveying cargoes from or to places as far west as Inverness on the one hand, and Banff on the other. These freights generally comprised material for building purposes, such as wood from the Spey and stones from "Cowsie." It was not unfrequently the case, too, that Dunbar, the proprietor of Nether Buckie, went down to the shore in the morning with a stick in his hand and drove the fishermen to sea, remarking that they would no doubt be able to find their way home again. He was interested in the boats going to sea because he obtained so many fish out of each catch. Cases occurred, too, where fishermen who did not go to sea often enough to please the laird were put in the "joogs," or manacled with irons. At the beginning of this century "joogs" were to be seen attached to the "Big Stane Hoose," which is situated on the east side of the Burn of Buckie. The fishermen at last refused to fulfil their bargains with the laird and several of them were put in the "joogs," with the result that about the year 1821 they commenced to build boats for themselves, and in the course of a few years thereafter the fishermen owned all the fishing boats.

Fishermen's Customs

The changes in manners and customs during the present century is extraordinary, but in no line of life has there been a greater change than in the manners and customs of the fishermen. To see a fishing boat now it is difficult to realise that it is not more than 32 years since all the boats were quite open, and had not a deck or a shelter of any kind for the crew. The first boat belonging to Buckie which was provided with a shelter was a boat which was launched in 1855, and was fitted up with a forecastle of a very primitive kind, and of very diminutive dimensions.

The fishermen in summer often went barefooted to sea, and wore a pair of canvas trousers and a huge "fear nothing" coat. Their underclothing and cap were of home-spun wool. It was only in the spring, when engaged in the great line fishing, that they even took a blanket to sea with them. For provisions they had some barley-meal bannocks, a roasted haddock or a pint or so of kail carried in a flagon, and perhaps they indulged occasionally in the luxury of an onion as "kitchy," all of which were rolled in a cloth and placed in a scull with the baited line. Each man had his berth on board, and it was with the greatest reluctance that he could be persuaded to assist his neighbour. The men in the midships had to bale the boat. One was situated in the "faren," and the other on the "aftern" side, and when on a long tack, if water was coming on board, the man on the lee side had a hard time of it baling while all his messmates looked on. When the tack was changed then the man who had been on the weather side had to bale, and his "spell" at this disagreeable duty would not be a long one if the boat was near the shore. There would be some danger of the boat completely filling before the crew would assist the men whose duty it was to bale.

Many of the large boats carried three masts - a foremast, mainmast, and mizzen, but no jib. The largest sail was in the centre of the boat, the next largest being the foresail. In stormy weather the mainmast was taken down and run over the stern. It was only very rarely before the forecastle was introduced into boats that the crews when at the line fishing stayed at sea all night; but lines being sometimes damaged during the darkness, and boats becoming more comfortable, reconciled fishermen to remain at sea until morning to protect their gear. The practice was for the crews to leave for the fishing at such an hour as would enable them to see both sides of the Firth when shooting their lines.

During the winter fishing each man required someone to bait his lines and assist him in hauling up and launching the boat for sea, and if his wife was unable to perform the duties owing to domestic cares he had to engage a female servant. In the morning the man who was first at the boat provided himself with a stone, and feeling in the darkness for the head of a nail he struck the nail with the stone, and this noisy process of summoning the crews was continued until the last laggard had arrived; some of the women, meanwhile, having been going from door to door to see that all the men and women concerned were awakened. At the launching and taking up of the boat the women stood side by side with their "masters," as the fishermen to whom they were engaged were called. When the boat was afloat the women had to hand on board the ballast and lines to the men, and it was not an unusual thing on a cold winter's day for them to be wet to the height of the waist. In Buckie and Portknockie, we are told, the practice of the women going to the shore was discontinued about the beginning of this century, what assistance was required for the boats being given by neighbours; but at the other places the practice was continued for a good many years later. Of course, when the boats were go to sea, the women had to got to gather mussels for bait; and on the return of the fishermen from sea the women were again at the shore. Occasionally they carried the men and lines ashore. It was often the case, however, that the fishermen were so wet that, in the words of our aged informant, it appeared as if they had "been dragged in the sea," and the matter of their wading or being carried ashore could not make much difference. Before the fish were apportioned - and each man getting his share - a certain number were selected for the women in lieu of wages. Having no time to clean and dispose of the fish the women generally took their "wages" to an old widow woman who cleaned the fish and undertook their sale, keeping a commission for her trouble and giving the fisher girls the balance when the time came for settling. The fish being taken from the shore were emptied on the middle of the floor of the dwellings, and the work of cleaning was proceeded with. It need scarcely be said that the performance of such an operation within the hovels which passed muster for houses in those days, did not tend at all to the cleanliness, comfort, or convenience of the inmates, any more than did the business in fish oil in which the fishermen engaged, the livers of the fish being kept in a barrel and afterwards made into oil for sale or barter.

The herring fishing commenced between the 18th and 20th of July, and continued for six weeks. Wick, at the beginning of this century, was the principal place to which

Banffshire boats went to engage in the herring fishing, but a number always remained at home. Several boats also generally went to Banff, Macduff, and Portsoy to fish. From 20 to 30 boats were usually fishing at Buckie. Portessie has had the honour of having at one time as many as 22 boats engaged in the herring fishing, which, at the time we write, was considered a great number. There was then no Continental markets for the sale of herrings, the fish being principally consigned to Ireland. The herrings were put into barrels, and were despatched by sloops and schooners which were frequently no larger than the present Zulu boats. The vessels lay at anchor close ashore, and the barrels were taken off in boats and put on board. The average cost of a freight to Ireland was 4s 6d per barrel, and it was sometimes the case that the fish lay as long in the Irish markets as they do now on the Continent before being sold. The price paid per barrel to the fishermen was from 7s to 10s. As an encouragement to the industry the Government paid 4s of bounty for every barrel of fish that was cured, which is a little different from now when 4d per barrel has to be paid for obtaining the Government brand. But even on the favourable terms which we have mentioned the fishcurers now and then had losses.

A good few consignments of herrings have been sent from Buckie to the West Indies. The fish were enclosed in barrels bound with iron hoops, and were taken to London for shipment. They were cured in the usual way, and having lain for eleven days were emptied out of the barrels in presence of the fishery officer, washed in pickle, and finally packed in barrels for transport. Each barrel contained 2 cwt. of herrings, to which 70 lbs. of Spanish salt of a reddish colour and considerable roundness was applied.

The Earliest Fishcurers

It may be here remarked that Buckie's connection with the herring fishing dates much further back than does the connection of Fraserburgh and Peterhead, and it is undoubtedly the case that the Buckie boats have contributed greatly to the history of Wick as a fishing station. Among the earliest fishcurers were Alexander Thomson, whose premises were near the shore of the present Nether Buckie or Buckpool harbour; Alexander Jamieson, whose yard was on the site of Mr Dick's house, near the Coastguard Station; Geddes and Ogilvie, who had premises at the Little Hythe; William Logie, who was to the east of the Coastguard Station, which was not then built; and the junior of the foregoing, and the last we need mention here, is Mr John Geddes, who began business in 1827, and whose premises were erected where the Coastguard Station has been since built. He served his apprenticeship with Messrs Geddes and Ogilvie, and is yet in good health, although several years ago he was compelled from declining strength to retire from business. In the course of a conversation with him one day he remarked that the herrings in the early years were of much better quality than those to be seen now, which he hold are caught too early. Three of the earliest Portgordon fishcurers, we may mention, were John Reid, George Stronach, and James Smith.

Catching herrings by daylight was not altogether unknown, in connection with which a little incident may be narrated. A Buckie boat was preparing to return home from the herring fishing at Wick when the crew heard that large quantities of herrings were being caught in a small sandy bay 15 miles to the north of Wick. They set out for the bay, which they reached about 11 o'clock in the forenoon, and observed great shoals of herrings piled thickly above each other with heads pointing downwards. The nets were shot, and were seen to move over the mass of almost immovable fish by the action of the tide, without dislodging or catching one; but now and then suddenly one of the "lumps" would start away and come full tilt against the net. Block and tackle would then be required to take it on board with the fish it contained, in addition to the spar or oar used when the nets were being hauled.

Haddocks from 1806 to 1812 were very plentiful in Buckie bay. On one occasion the crew of a small boat caught so many that it became a serious question whether the boat would ever reach land. The corpulent personage who steered was ordered to go to the bow, which was highest out of the water, but this did not at all improve matters. However the men with their big take got safely to the shore. Such a large catch of haddocks that the boat has to be trimmed to a nicety is unknown in these latter days. The small boats at this time, it may be mentioned, were from 16 to 18 feet of keel, and carried four of a crew.

Keith Market

The herring fishing closed the fishermen seldom went to sea until after the Keith market (which was held in September), and the lifting of the potatoes. Every fisherman, it may be here remarked, had at least half an acre of ground, in the cultivation of which he obtained the services of small crofters near the town. For the ground 7s 6d to 10s was paid, the yearly rent paid for the boat obtained from the laird including the rent of the site of the fishermen's dwelling-houses. The Keith market was a right Royal holiday for the fisherfolk, who trooped to Keith in crowds. Numerous purchases were made, but in particular every three or four families joined in buying an animal, which was taken on to Buckie and killed to provide flesh meat for the winter. The average price paid for a beast was from £4 to £5.

The haddock fishing which followed the herring fishing, was continued till the month of January, and from that month till March was occupied in preparation for the great line fishing, consequently "the back of Eel" was known as the "barest time of all the year" to the fisher population.

Disposing of Fish

During the winter the fishermen went to Inverness, Dingwall, and other places in the Firth for the purpose of disposing of the oil which had been obtained from the haddock and cod livers, and brought back bark for dyeing the nets, and other things that they may have required. At the smaller places where the boats called to dispose of their oil - which was principally used for lamps, of course - it was not unusual for the parish church bell to be set aringing to intimate the fact, and the intelligence of the arrival of a Buckie boat with oil flew inland like wildfire. Boats even went to Inverallochy, Rosehearty, and other places to the east for the purpose of purchasing oil and dogfish to take to the west to sell. The rate at which the oil was sold was from 16s to 20s per anker of 20 pints. Dogfish, it may be remarked, was a favourite food, so much so that at Rosehearty and adjoining fishing villages dogs and haddocks were the only fishings which the fishermen regularly engaged in, the prosecution of the herring fishing being left to the Banffshire boats. Dogfish are now despised, but then they were carefully dried and eaten unsalted.

At the beginning of this century a crew of eight or nine men had three sizes of boats at their command. For the herring and haddock fishing the second largest boat was considered sufficient, and measured from 28 to 32 feet of keel. She was the property of the fishermen, as were also the small boats which were mostly used at the haddocks at the end of the herring fishing. The boats used for the great-line fishing were a foot or two larger than the herring boats, and were the property of the lairds. Owing to the nature of the work an increase of one or two hands to the crew was the rule. Fifty years ago the price of a boat of 30 to 32 feet of keel with 12 feet 4 inches of beam, and a depth of 5 feet 2 inches was £25.

About the latter end of May the fishermen took a second trip to dispose of the fruits of their toil, and on this occasion proceeded to Leith, Glasgow, and even to England and Ireland. What they carried was principally dried fish.

CHAPTER IV

Superstition

*I*t must be confessed that along the coast of Banffshire superstition was as rampant as it was possible for it to be, haunting its victims with the closest attention by day and by night. The fishermen said that when they went out in the morning a beast known to them by the name of "cockie-coo" came and took off their bonnets; and had they been asked where they were going as they were proceeding to their boats for the purpose of going to sea, the likelihood is that they would have turned back and remained on shore all day. Had the enquirer been a youth, who had asked the question out of mischief, very likely he would have been chased and got a thrashing. At anyrate, "Old Bowie," a cooper, threw a net off his back and pursued an urchin through Buckie, and administered chastisement to him for merely asking where he was going. Not only did the fishermen dislike to have such a question asked of them, but they were also in terror when going to their boats that they would meet anyone who was "ill-fitted" (i.e., had an evil foot), because if they did so they were sure that they would at least get no fish that day, if actual calamity did not befall them. "Gracious Guides!" - a favourite ejaculation of Willie Geddes "Jockles," who resided on the top of the brae at Nether Buckie - was uttered with great consternation by "Jockles" one morning when he suddenly came face to face with Sandy Sclater, who was accounted "ill-fitted."

A worthy dame who resided in Portessie, and was in the habit of going to the country to dispose of her fish, had the misfortune to live next door to a diminutive man named Simpson, who was a quiet inoffensive person, but was considered "ill-fitted." The consequence was that she felt it incumbent upon her to rise particularly early in the morning to get a-field before there was a likelihood of meeting the object of her aversion. One morning she set forth, but had not gone far when she met Simpson, and thought it advisable to return home, where she arrived in a state of indignation and excitement. After a while she made a second attempt to proceed on her journey, and took a route which she thought would be unlikely to bring Simpson athwart her course, but she had just got round the corner of a house when she came full tilt upon him, and thereupon assailed him with abuse until the poor man actually trembled in his shoes. With gloomy brow she proceeded on her journey, and disposed of her fish for meal and other necessaries of life. On her return she was asked how she got on, to which she replied - "I weel kent how I would get on when I met yon warl's wonner."

In Portknockie, especially, even dogs were considered "ill-fitted," and it is narrated of one fisherman who, when he met a dog when going to sea, pursued it until he had caught it, and thereupon killed it. Hares and rabbits, too, were held in the greatest abhorrence all along the coast; and to have found a hare, rabbit, or salmon on board a boat would most certainly have prevented the fishermen from going to sea that day.

A fisherman named Mair "Shavie." who resided at Portknockie, had in the boat with him a hired man named Paterson. In taking the nets to dry Paterson's house had to be passed, and Mair "Shavie" saw with secret annoyance that Paterson's children kept rabbits. The fishing proving unsuccessful, Mair took it into his head that connection with rabbits was at the bottom of their bad luck, and Paterson was told to leave. He was, however, soon engaged by another skipper named Wood, and one day they arrived at Portknockie with a heavy shot of herrings. Paterson was well aware of Mair's superstitious ideas, and confronting him he drew from his breast a hare's skin, and shaking it in Mair's face, said - "That is the thing that has the luck." Mair evidently thought that the bad luck which had attended him had been owing to Paterson's connection with rabbits, and that his hired man had intentionally kept them from getting herrings. The fish that Wood caught he considered were those he had been deprived of through Paterson's artifice. In a great rage, therefore, he went down to the beach and desired Wood to hand him over the fish, and even wanted his sons and others to take them by force.

About seventy years ago a very superstitious fisherman known by the name of "Bouffie," resided in Buckie. His predilections were well known, and on one occasion a number of young men belonging to Portgordon determined to play a joke upon him. Procuring a hare's skin the jokers filled it with rubbish, and placed it near the stern of the boat of which "Bouffie" was skipper, where he could readily see it on proceeding to sea. It was the time of the herring fishing, and as the boat was leaving for sea "Bouffie" caught sight of the hare's skin and ejaculated that they were long enough in a boat that they was accursed by having a hare's skin on board. Persuasion was used with the view of getting him to go to sea, but all without avail, and he informed his crew that if they did so they would most certainly not be seen again. They, however, evidently knowing about the joke, went off to the fishing, "Bouffie" watching them with gloomy face and shaking his head ominously, fervently believing that neither boat nor men would ever be séen again. To his relief, but greatly to his mortification at the same time, the boat arrived on the following day with a fair catch of herrings. "Bouffie"had his superstitious beliefs shaken a good bit, but it was a long time before he recovered from the shock he received at what he thought the unaccountable escape of his mates from certain death.

The fishermen had the greatest antipathy to certain names being mentioned when at sea. Salmon, rats, hares, and rabbits, durst not be spoken about, and anyone who talked about clergymen was sure to be hissed by way of warning. Ross was a name which was greatly detested, and when anyone of that name was referred to at sea he was spoken of as "chuff 'em oot." The Cullen fishermen, besides having an aversion like their Buckie brethren to the name of Ross, considered that to mention the name of Anderson and Duffus at sea also brought ill-luck, and spoke of the former as "the man who sells the coals."

Buckie fisherman who, unlike most of his brethren, was not at all tainted with superstitious beliefs, was going to sea with a brother-in-law who resided at Portknockie. While they were sailing off to the herring fishing one day the Buckie fisherman resolved to play a little joke on his relative. He asked the name of the builder of the boat, and was met with a vague answer that it was a man in Cullen. The Buckie fisherman was well aware who had built the boat, and as it happened to be a person of the detested name of Ross he was endeavouring to get his brother-in -law to pronounce it. To all the questions put, vague answers were given, the replies being that it was not such and such a one, but a man who resided at a place which was described. Finding that all efforts to get his sister's husband to pronounce the name was useless, with mischief in his heart and a grave face he said - "Oh, then, it must be Ross." The Portknockie fisherman gazed in horror at he who had dared to utter such a name on board of a boat, and held up his hands and exclaimed, "Oh, God forgee ye," adding that they would get no fish that night. A pretty good haul of herring was secured, however, which made a fitting subject for jokes at the expense of the Portknockie fisherman.

The time was when only wooden pins were used for thowels. Each pin was made of hard wood so that it might stand the strain of an oar in rowing, and every fisherman who rowed an oar had always two, which were marked with an initial letter, and of so much value were they considered that they were taken home at night in the scull. On one occasion at the shore of Portessie a pin was accidently dropped into the water and not missed at the time by the owner. It was drifting out to sea when it was seen by one of the crew of a boat that was moored off the shore to keep her afloat, and was picked up by him. The season wore on, and the boat on which the lost pin was made a good fishing, while the one that had lost the pin did almost nothing. It at last became known that the successful boat had the missing pin, and a fierce and bitter animosity arose amongst the Smiths, Gardens, and Farquhars of the village, and numerous fights took place. The party who lost the pin held that it had been stolen for the purpose of taking away the luck of the boat and giving it to the boat on board which it was taken, and this idea was held to be justified by events. The dispute did not abate till the pin had been returned, and an explanation made that it had been found, and not wilfully stolen. The incident, however, aptly illustrates the extraordinary superstition of the times.

A crew of old men fishing from Buckie were in the habit of spitting upon a piece of bent or sea-ware and throwing it overboard when their lines got entangled at the bottom. This act, it was thought, facilitated the unfastening of the line.

There were parties, too, who were accredited with having an "evil eye," and when such a serious operation as the dyeing of wool in the wool or in the yarn was to take place, it was customary for the gudewife to lock the door, and screen the window so that no "evil eye" could see the operations and prevent the wool from taking on the dye properly.

There was a curious idea among the seafaring people with regard to New Year's Day. On the first morning of every year they went down to the shore and filled a small flagon with salt water, and also took some sea-ware. The water was then strewn about the fire, and the ware was put upon the top of the doors.

Another superstitious belief was that no fire should be given out of the house on a New Year's morning, anent which a little incident may be narrated. On a New Year's morning a fisherman who resided near Bridge End met a boy coming out of his house as usual with a piece of lighted turf for the purpose of kindling a fire in a shoemaker's workshop. In greatest wrath the fisherman abused his wife for having allowed the lad to take away the fire, stating that he would not be able to catch a fish that year. The fisherman had never been successful at the fishing, but at the winter cod fishing he was the most successful of all the boats, and at the ensuing summer herring fishing, as if entirely to crush his foolish superstitious notions out of his head, his was amongst the best fished boats. Afterwards the lad twitted Willie, for such was the fisherman's Christian name, at being so angry at him taking away the fire, whereupon Willie said he would never quarrel with anybody again for doing so, and wished that the lad would come every day as usual and get a light for his fire. Willie, however, was not cured of all his superstitious beliefs by this incident.

It will be news to numbers that there are some medicinal properties or other virtue in an ordinary shilling - at least, such was thought to be the case. When anyone was ill, or was supposed to be "forespoken," or labouring under the spell of someone with an evil eye, it was customary to drop a shilling in a cog of water, and give the patient a draught of this magical decoction with the very greatest solemnity. Further, if when the water was poured off, the shilling remained in the bottom of the cog, then the sick party was to live; but if it did not stick to the bottom, then there was to be a death, and the relatives had no time to lose in sending off to Paris for the latest fashions in mourning!

Then, too, it was very unlucky for the lamp to burn on the side of the house on which the line was being baited; and it was not lucky to leave the ladle in the kail pot when the lid was upon it.

A treasure in almost every household was a piece of fir stick from which a knot had been ejected, leaving a hole through the wood. When a girl got married such a piece of wood was ignited and the anxious mother-in-law performed the ceremony of describing a circle round the head of the bride with the stick. Such a piece of wood was also said to be useful for driving away fairies and other elves, and before a child was born a circle was described round the mother with the "candle fir" to prevent the fairies from stealing the child. A dead body was treated in a similar manner, for it seems the fairies took the dead as well as the living. When the ceremony of the lighted stick was going on, the performer said:- "I'm sayin' ye, in the name of the Father, Son, and Holy Ghost." Night and day a candle was burned beside a dead body, and a green sod and tobacco were laid on the corpse.

From what has already been said it will have been seen that a hundred years ago there was a pretty widespread belief in fairies. All the burns in the district were said to be infested with these sprites, who, when they got hold of mortals, kept them in custody for a year. One incident of this kind is narrated. A young man in Nether Buckie was sent by his father for a "chappin" of ale, and did not return for a year, having during that time been the companion of fairies. Evidence of the existence of fairies was given by a worthy dame who lived, we know not how many years ago. She was on one occasion at the Mill of Gollachy having her corn ground, and had been detained until twelve o'clock at night. Just as she came to the crossing of the road she heard the most seraphic music ever she listened to coming from the direction of "the haughs" and saw a whole regiment of fairies, most picturesquely dressed, singing and carrying some of their number in state, as if it was a funeral procession. The woman hurried to get across the road before the fairies came up, which she succeeded in doing, and arrived safely at home much frightened.

We have it on the authority of people who have heard it from other people, that fairies did not confine themselves to the dells and glens, but made themselves at home in human habitations, and in particular were fond of frequenting the small house which stood on the site of the Cluny Hotel, and was occupied by the widow of a buccaneer captain who is said to have been quartered. At anyrate, the building was popularly believed to be haunted.

A Witchcraft Trial

Stories of witchcraft can also be narrated. An interesting witchcraft trial is to be found in the extracts of the minutes of the Presbytery of Fordyce, published by Mr Crammond. Fortunately, the story has not so tragic an ending as in the case of the man who laughed in kirk at Peterhead, and was burnt at the stake because he said he saw the devil sitting on the rafters.

On the 11th of November, 1656, Margaret Philp, spouse to Gilbert Imblaughe, dwelling near Cullen, was apprehended and tried in the Tolbooth at Cullen for the crime of witchcraft. The presiding judge was "Mr Johne Abercrombie, one of the Justices of the Peace for the Sherefdome of Banff," who met with Mr James Chalmer, Presbyterian minister of Cullen, and the elders of the burgh. The result of the trial was that the woman was set at liberty, much to the dissatisfaction of the minister of Cullen, who brought the case before a meeting of the Presbytery on the 13th of January, 1657. On the 18th of the following month Mr Chalmer submitted to the Presbytery evidence which had been adduced at the trial. The principal witness for the prosecution was an "Isobel Imblaughe, spouse to James Duffus in Forsken, ane married woman of the age of thretie-six yeirs." The affair was thus likely a family one. Being solemnly sworn she deponed that she heard Isobel Imblaughe, sometime a servant with Mrs Imblaughe, confess that about midday when "the Spirit was raging about" Mrs Imblaughe's house, a beast like a hare came in. Isobel directed the attention of Mrs Imblaughe to the hare, who replied - "Fool thing, let it alone; I see nothing." Mrs Duffus further said that the Isabel Imlah who saw this also told her that "the Spirit" said - "Give me that 'gleyd' witch, Maggie Soullie, for she is mine." This remark was repeated twice or thrice. A remark which criminated Mrs Imblaughe still further was the statement of "the Spirit" to her - "Remember thou not that thou and I did sail in the riddle together in the 'fleuck pot' with several others, whereof Margaret Clark, Marjorie Kelman, and Janet Cuy were a part of our number."

Isabel Imblaughe, being examined, acknowledged that she had repeated to Mrs Duffus the statements adduced, and that she saw the hare drinking water in an inner chamber and dancing upon "ane koppe." The hare was finally seen to go through the window "lyk ane cload." In relation to "the Spirit's" statement about "Maggie Soullie," (Maggie's soul?) Isabel stated that the Spirit further remarked that "Maggie Soullie" had been his "thir four sewen yers." She further "confessed" that Mrs Imblaughe said - "Avoid, Satan, common lying thief." She also mentioned that "the Spirit" sought meat from Margaret, who put a bannock, a drink of water, and a piece of flesh into "ane ambrie," and that Mrs Imblaughe said -"This is the Spirit." She confessed also that Margaret acknowledged that the bannock, flesh, and water were gone next morning; and that "the Spirit" had taken the key of her pantry door from her breast when she was drinking in John Mennie's house, and that she unfastened her clothes and searched in several places for it until "the Spirit" informed her that he had returned it to the place from whence he had taken it, and there she found it. Mrs Imblaughe said to "the Spirit" - "Tak' you Helen Runcie."

Evidently "the Spirit" was in love with Mrs Imblaughe, for he replied - "I will have none of your choosing. I will have only you." "The Spirit"further added - "Henry Philp's ghost spak' but two nights to thee. Thou then raised me."

Isabel went on to say that she heard "the Spirit" remark that Mrs Imblaughe promised her "ane prey," and having mentioned Thomas Imblaughe, son to Gilbert Imblaughe, heard the said Gilbert declare, - "Thou has no power over me nor none of mine; to whom "the Spirit" replied - "I have power over Soullie, witch, thy wife."

This seems to have ended the conference with "the Spirit," and at the close Mrs Imblaughe threatened Isabel not to declare what she had heard or seen, as if she did so it would be the worse for her, as she would likely be confined a prisoner in "the joogs" and subjected to the ridicule and the abuse of the whole town

Gilbert Imblaughe, who was sixty years old, was next examined, and confirmed the evidence of Isabel Imblaughe, the last witness, only he denied having heard his wife threaten her if she declared what she had seen and heard.

The accused, Margaret Philp or Imblaughe, was also examined, and confessed that the voice that spoke to her was that of the devil. The devil warned her that although she behaved herself as well as she could, he would have her at the last; and intimated that he and she were to sail in a riddle that night. All the other accusations she acknowledged to be strictly true.

Whether the whole thing was a plot of Mrs Imblaughe's servant or not, it is somewhat suspicious that "the Spirit" commanded Mrs Imblaughe to buy five ells of plaiding, and a head-dress and pins for the Isobel Imblaughe who spread the story, which she did.

The Presbytery having considered the foregoing depositions, ordained the Rev. James Chalmer to summarily excommunicate Mrs Imblaughe and report.

CHAPTER V

Mollusc Eaters

*A*msterdam is said to be founded on herring bones. The older parts of Buckie are literally built on shells. Excavations often reveal deposits of shells several feet in depth, which, to the conchologist, would prove a rich and instructive mine. These deposits consist chiefly of molluscs of the whelk and bucky type, mixed frequently with pieces of broken delfware. Such accumulations speak silently of the many generations of mollusc eaters that have lived and died unrecorded save by these faithful historians. Palatable and nutritious dishes of shellfish were cooked almost daily by Buckie grandmothers, a branch of cookery which has become obsolete if not altogether lost.

We can safely take it for granted that the first fishers did not venture further than what the great spring tide left bare. Then, as time passed, and pressing necessity made them use the skin-covered vessel, or the canoe scooped from the solid tree, we can almost trace step by step the various improvements down to the modern painted and gilded Zulu.

The employment of Fishermen on Shore

The industrious fisherman was never out of employment. He got little or no assistance from mechanical inventions. The day of these helps had not yet dawned. Nearly everything was hand made. No later than 100 years ago the fishermen of Portessie even made all the lines and ropes they required, and a few in Buckie also did so, there being only one ropemaker in the district, and he resided at Cullen. All the fishermen made their own sails, and there are those alive who have seen the operation performed. Then hook-making, which was a very tedious process, was also engaged in, and amongst the other duties the fishermen employed themselves at when ashore were mounting lines, making sneeds, hair tippends, osals, sculls, creels, and baskets, as also repairing sails, and splicing ropes. Some of the old men almost made the different kinds of splicing works of art. Now and then houses had to be built, or re-thatched, so that there was little time for idleness. Then in the long winter evenings, when the wind howled and whistled round the small thatched houses, by the murky flames of the "shally" oil lamp or equally defective candle, the women made or repaired nets, while the old grandfather told stories of long ago, to which all his auditors listened with breathless attention. Now he told of some disastrous storm, and miraculous escapes and fatal disasters; or narrated strange stories of murders or encounter with the supernatural, or striking omens of coming disaster - omens that were faithfully fulfilled - and as the rain dashed upon the small window pane, or the wind shook the stout door or roared down the chimney, the younger listeners shuddered and gazed apprehensively into the corners of the room but dimly illuminated by the flickering light of the lamp and fire. These were never-to-be-forgotten nights, and left their eerie influence on the young listeners, and cultivated and handed down from sire to son all sorts of superstitious notions.

Then in the dimness of the falling night how the boys loved to chase each other round the houses that stood in higgeldy - piggeldy order, as if set down for the purpose of affording them a good game at hide and seek! But the houses were not built to suit the young folk, there being order in the very disorder, for the object aimed at was to obtain shelter from 'the cauld blasts.' Perhaps the youthful fun was increased by tormenting some old and crusty woman who might be considered "ill-fitted," or even a witch; or by arousing the wrath of some old cross-grained and "ill-fitted" man. With what terror, too, did the boys all the time play up their pranks, in case they should be seen by the party at whose door they were mischievously knocking, or down whose chimney they were throwing stones, sods, and dead cats! They dreaded to be seen by the parties whom they were tormenting, in case they should fall under the spell of their diabolical arts. Aye, those were rare times, heightened by the absence of the modern "bobbies." Then there were stone fights, when the "Cully" (Easter Buckie) fisher boys battled against the "Yanter" (Nether Buckie) boys, or when the fisher boys fought the trades boys. In the former case the Burn of Buckie often divided the combatants, but in the latter the hay ricks in the vicinity of the site of the U.P. Church formed a rare spot for the generalship of the commanders of the respective youthful parties. Then the Buckie boys at Rathven School were always at drawn daggers with the boys of Findochty, and often the Buckie force, to the number of 20 to 30, drove their opponents back on their supports, the houses of Findochty.

The Fishermen's Knowledge of their Craft

The fishermen of "days of yore" had little book learning, but it is sturdily contended that they were far in advance of the present generation in the study of Nature. All their doings were regulated by natural phenomena. Lacking the aids of the weather indicators of the present day the sky was studied, as also the state of the atmosphere, and the appearance of the surface of the sea.These enabled them to make fairly correct weather forecasts for the next 24 hours at least. But the absence of a deeper knowledge often leads to many grave misconceptions, hence the rise of many forms of superstition. One of the most remarkable characteristics of the fishermen 80 years ago and more, we are told, was their intimate acquaintance with the fishing ground. The Moray Firth is said to be one of the best spawning grounds known. The bottom is thickly marked by low rocky reefs. Over these banks, as they were called, shoals of fish are generally to be found. These fish resorts are, or at least were, quite familiar, and as each bank had a distinctive name the fishermen spoke of where they caught their last shot of fish with the same familiarity as one would speak of a well-known town or street, and could sail to any given spot with the utmost certainty. The features of the land were their guides.

When a fisherman asked where a more successful friend got a good haul, the reply would be at Tarbet Ness, on the Gelim Bank or, if nearer home, on the Hattie, Coarl, or Half o' Coral, Hill Grun; or, if further from land, the Craig, the Edge of Deep, Deep Water, etc. Not only could they go to the different shot heads, but were also acquainted with the nature of the bottom by what came up on their lines or nets when they had been on the ground. The present investigations into the habits and food of the creatures of the mighty deep are confirming many of the old ideas on the subject. It is not intended to under-rate the knowledge of the young fishermen of the present day, but it is contended that in weather lore, in intimate acquaintance with the fishing ground, and in the vagaries of the finny tribes, individual knowledge is on the decrease. But there is a reason. The whole fishing industry has undergone a great change during the past fifty years. Fishermen are often from home, engaged chiefly in the herring fishing at different parts of the coast, and are becoming quite strange to what was so familiar and needful to their elders. Though these early fishermen now and again suffered terrible disasters, they were undoubtedly hardy and brave. Their greatest fear was that they should be caught by a storm in the Skate Hole in their open boats, with nothing to shelter them from the fierceness of the elements, and only a limited supply of provisions aboard, generally more or less soaked with salt water. When caught in a gale, and the wind had died suddenly away, leaving a mountainous sea and the boats at the mercy of the waves, on several occasions crews have fastened skate and turbot to the oars, and suspended them as high as they could to catch all the wind possible. When a change of tack was necessary the fish were dropped into the sea and others put up on the other side of the boat.

The Skate Hole was first discovered and obtained its name , it is said, from an incident. While the barracks at Fort George were being built, the contractor engaged the Nairn fishermen to catch skate from which to obtain oil. Skate oil was held to be the best for mixing with cement, and good takes of skate being obtained at what is now known as the Skate Hole it obtained its present name.

The Press Gang

During the troublous latter half of the last century and the beginning of the present century, a large proportion of the Buckie seafaring men were, either by voluntary enlistment or by the aid of the press gang, found in the fighting ranks of His Majesty, but chiefly in the navy. Whether it is to their credit or not it is said that there were one or two Buckie men had a hand in the famous incident of "tapping the Admiral." The few that ever returned home again brought back not only pocketfuls of prize money, but improved ideas of their calling. Instead of doing most of their work by sheer physical strength, as formerly, they had learned and induced their old companions to use labour-saving mechanical appliances, in the shape of improved pulleys and tackling. The impulse given, the fishing industry has ever since then made steady progress.

Numerous incidents might be given in connection with the press gang. On one occasion an old Buckie fisherman and his wife were proceeding south in a boat to dispose of fish. They were the entire crew if we except a litter of young dogs. The boat, it is said, was thus badly manned owing to the havoc that had been caused among the male population by the press gang. In the course of the voyage the old man saw with no pleasant feelings a coasting cruiser ahead of him lowering a boat for the purpose of overhauling his craft to see if there were any subjects on board suitable for His Majesty's navy. The old man held on his course, and succeeded in running down the boat, when the enraged boat's crew boarded him and took him and his boat in custody. He was taken to Leith, and brought up in court for trial. Side by side with him was his wife, and in his arms he held the scull containing the litter of young dogs. To the great amusement of all in court with the utmost gravity he repeated the charge to the pups, pretending to think that they were also charged with the offence. The scene grew so comical that the wily fisherman was discharged.

It is narrated that during the time of the press gang, a boat was seen to be pursued by a cutter. The boat ran ashore near where the present Coastguard Station is, and immediately half-a-dozen men, dressed like fishermen, sprang ashore and ran up the brae. An old woman, known as Bell Saun'ers, who was credited with being partly insane, invited the men to enter her little cottage, which still stands at the top of the brae. They accepted the invitation, and the door being closed, the woman hid them in her bed. Thereupon she threw a quantity of fish livers and sea ware on the fire , from which was emitted a dense smoke of an intolerable stench. The cutter had meantime lowered a boat, which, filled with armed men, was rapidly rowed to the shore. The cutter's men landing, followed their prey up the brae, having observed that they had disappeared among the houses. The houses were searched for the fugitives, and on coming to Bell Saunders' door one man opened it and peered in. Seated by the fire he observed Bell with intentionally dishevelled locks over her brow. The smoke and smell caused him rapidly to retreat, and his motions were accelerated by the fact that the woman rose up and behaved like a thorough lunatic, and as if she would tear him to pieces. The man's companions coming up he informed them that there was no one in the house but an insane old woman. A peep in at the doorway was sufficient to overcome the zeal of the most indefatigable, and the search party passed on. During the night several women escorted the pursued men up the country and along the foot of the hills to Cullen. It is stated that the men, from their speech and deportment, were not fishermen, and it was conjectured that they belonged to the west coast and were refugees of some sort. At anyrate, it is said that the men exceedingly handsomely rewarded with gold pieces the women of the Seatown who rendered them any assistance, many of them consequently rising from poverty to comparative affluence. The visit of the strangers was consequently a noteworthy event, and was the subject of much speculation for a long time.

More about the Herring Fishing

The catching of herring by nets is ascribed by tradition to the seventeenth century, during which some men from the Firth of Forth came to the district and taught the art of catching herring by means of nets. One reason why the south coast fishermen of the Moray Firth have become so distinguished in the capture of fish is that the bays of the Firth are almost unsurpassed in Great Britain as spawning grounds and hence the stories of extraordinary catches of fish in days of yore, when the fishing material was of such a kind as would be considered almost worthless at the present time. In the main, the manner of fishing is still the same as it was eighty and a hundred years ago, but the appliances have so outgrown the original as to seem altogether different. The small open boats, though not to be compared with those of the present day, were quite large enough for their crews, when it is remembered that they had to be hauled up at every appearance of a change of weather, and launched again when the storm was over. This was a very serious undertaking, especially if there were no a sufficient number of persons present. It is said that there was hardly a fisherman who had not experienced the pain of fractured bones or injured spine, received in the operation of moving the boats. The fishcurers, it may be remarked, only cured herrings and haddock, and one or two of them perhaps cured a few cod. Among the other duties of the fishermen was that of carrying the fish to the fishcuring yards. They were also in the habit of taking their nets almost daily to the grass to dry, instead of once a week as at present. At sea it always required skilled seamanship on the part of the skippers to guide the operation of "shooting" the nets, they being placed parallel to each other.

Lights at Sea

When the evenings were cold some of the boats carried an old iron pot to be used for the purpose of containing a fire; but the success of lighting a fire at sea was so uncertain that most of the crews dispensed with this comfort altogether rather than waste their time over it. Of the several ancient means of lighting , the tinder box may be considered the best of all. The "box" was generally a cow's horn filled with charred linen, prepared by the men's wives. The "flourish" was a small piece of steel about two inches long, with an ornamental curve at the end to hold it by, and was applied sharply to a piece of flint with a sharp angle. When the operator desired to strike a light he took off the cork stopper from the tinder box, and placed the box between his knees in a sitting position. Taking the flourish in one hand and the flint in the other he struck the flint causing sparks to fly in all directions till a spark fell on the dry tinder, which instantly began to smoulder. This was blown upon, and a flame was the result. But the greatest difficulty was to transfer the flame to light a fire in the pot. The chief use of the tinder box was to light the lantern or the tobacco pipe. Long after the introduction of the lucifer match many old fishermen preferred to light their pipes from the tinder boxes because of the more pleasant flavour it gave to the tobacco.

The lantern then used would be a very interesting object now-a-days. It was generally a square wooden box with small holes cut in three side, the fourth side being used as the "door" for giving access to the interior. These holes were filled with pieces of transparent horn, for glass was then a rather expensive article for general use. While the boat was riding at the nets the lantern was placed on the "midship back," with the dark side opposite to the direction from which the wind was blowing, no danger being apprehended from that quarter, as it was not possible for a sailing vessel to go far against the wind. These lights were only seen at short distances, but were the best that could be had, and served the purpose until candles and clearer glass came into general use.

The nets in these olden times were incapable of taking small or young fish, owing to the size of the mesh, which had to be made large because the hemp contracted greatly, and in a year or two became so blunt by the twine swelling that new nets had to be procured. These nets were very strong, and seldom broke with weight of fish, being in this respect superior to cotton ones. They were also smaller and a good deal heavier than the cotton ones.

It need scarcely be said that when Highlanders first began to be employed on board the boats as hired men they travelled most of the way on foot, often from the extreme end of Skye, the journey occupying them a week and more. Often they did not know a word of English. They carried a small bundle of clothes slung at their back over a stick until they had obtained an engagement. The wages they received were then a mere fraction of what is paid now, yet what they earned at the herring fishing was nearly all the money these poor people saw until next herring fishing. Their want of knowledge of English caused them to be looked upon pretty much as foreigners, and consequently fights between them and the local fishermen were not unfrequent.

Clothing and Food

The general dress of the working classes was of home-made stuff of a blue colour. It was a very rare thing to see a cloth coat upon anyone. Of course, the fashionable suit of the day was knee breeches and coat to suit, with shoes on which there were silver buckles. An old man who was born in the second year of this century remembers seeing his father set out for the church of Rathven, of which he was an elder, arrayed in the costume of the period - knee breeches, etc. - carrying a long stick with an ornamental head, and wearing a Scotch blue bonnet 18 inches broad, with a huge red tassle in the centre. At the beginning of this century the fishermen had got generally accustomed to the luxury of wearing shoes, which were worn until they were in a most dilapidated condition. They were fortunate children who got one pair of shoes in a year. The purchase was generally made at the beginning of winter, and there are those alive, indeed, who have seen fisher children sliding barefooted, and with the greatest glee, upon ice. These children, we are told, wore anything - that is, their outer attire would have been perhaps an old coat belonging to their father, or a gown that was past service for their mother. Now the fishermen are better dressed when they go to sea than what they were when going to church. Indeed, many of them could not go to church for want of proper clothing. The first seaboots used in this quarter, we believe, were made about 60 years ago, and for some years thereafter the shoemaker who made three or four pairs in a year thought he was doing a big business. There were then only five shoemakers in Buckie. Now, 70 to 80 pairs, with many more shoemakers in the town, are thought nothing unusual.

Barley meal cakes were the general bread, oatmeal being little known about, and consequently an oatmeal cake was a great luxury. Sixty to eighty years ago there was only one baker - Mackenzie - in Buckie. He baked penny loaves or "baps" made of flour, and did a pretty good business, his profits enabling him to build the house in Nether Buckie tenanted by Mr Paterson. grocer. Latterly, loaves were brought from Elgin until the number of bakers in the town was increased. It may here be said that the bread supplied by bakers is not nearly so good as the bread made by many English housewives. Milk, kail, turnips, fish, and potatoes were all pretty plentiful during this century, and tea was never an altogether unknown beverage. The first tea seen in Findochty was said to have been boiled like kail, and eaten afterwards. The tea was procured from a vessel, a brig, which went ashore at Findochty on the site of the present harbour, and for a good many years served as a pier by which the fishermen boarded their boats. Consequently, the place on which the vessel lay came to be known by the name of "The Brig." Tobacco, we are told, was never any cheaper than what it is now, being purchased at the rate of 3d and 3 1/2d an ounce. Spirituous liquors of all kinds, of course, were cheap, seeing that smuggling was engaged in to a considerable extent.

CHAPTER VI

Age of Rottenslough

We mentioned that Portessie, or Rottenslough, became a fishing station in 1727. This interesting locality, however, has rejoiced in the name of Rottenslough for now nearly three centuries at least, as the following extract from the Burgh Records of Cullen shows:- "1594, May 15th. Johannes Coull, ballivus, in hac parte Mri. Jocobi Haye, feoditarii de Rophane accessit personaliter ad vnam bouatam in dimidio bouate terrarum in Loneheid modo occupatarum per Andream Coull et ad vnam akirram tere jacentem in occidentali parte torrentis de Rophane ac etiam ad portum symbarum vocatum Rottinsloucht," which may be thus translated:- "John Coull baillie constituted of Mr James Hay fear of Rathven personally approached to a bovat of land in the half bovat of the lands of Lonehead lately occupied by Andrew Coull, and to an acre of land lying on the west side of the Burn of Rathven, and also to the boat-hythe called Rottinslough."

Carriers' Carts and Mail Coaches

Things have changed greatly in Buckie since the time when the carriers' carts journeyed to Aberdeen. The carriers generally left on Monday morning, and usually had a good load of haddocks for disposal in the Granite City. They brought back goods, arriving on Friday night, and delivering their boxes and packages on the following day. Some of the carts went by Keith and Huntly, and others by Banff, Turriff, and Old Meldrum. There was no changing of horses on the journey, and when the carrier put up for the night he depended on his dog to guard the goods which were under his charge. The nearest coach stations were at Fochabers and Keith, Buckie not being of sufficient importance for any of the passenger coaches from the west to come out of the way to obtain its custom. The fare from Fochabers and Keith to Aberdeen, on the outside of the coach, was half-a-guinea. At every station, said one of our informants, the driver expected to receive a "tip" from each of the passengers, and if he did not get this he abused worse than a pickpocket those who failed to give him money. A "tip"of a shilling at a time was considered a very small honorarium. Journeys on foot in those days, however, were more often resorted to than were the coaches, luggage being sent on by the carriers. Doubtless it would not be very difficult at the present moment to get half a dozen persons in Buckie who have travelled on foot to and from Aberdeen. The travellers pretty often proceeded across the country by the west shoulder of the Bin Hill, and, if fair walkers, were generally in Aberdeen before the carriers who were conveying their luggage.

First Iron Plough

At the beginning of the century the land lying between the road leading to the Tollbar and the Burn of Freuchny was a moor of whins and broom. About the year 1826, however, an iron plough was sent from Cluny with four oxen for the purpose of reclaiming the ground, and this was ultimately accomplished. The plough was the first iron one seen in the district, and it created quite a sensation. When it had accomplished its work it was put into a barn at the Cluny Stables, on the south-west corner of Low Street. The barn is now in ruins, and the plough lies amongst the debris. It is exceedingly heavy, and is a model of the old wooden plough. The land to the farm of Mains of Buckie on the west side of the road leading to the Tollbar was also a moor at the same time.

Tarbuckie

At the back of West Church Street may be seen a house in the midst of arable land. It is occupied by Mr Farquhar, and indicates the site of the village of Tarbuckie. The village at the beginning of the century was composed of 12 families. Farquhar's house was on the opposite side (the north) of the road from the abodes of the other villagers, and he and his family were consequently known as "the tribe beyond the Jordan." The whole of the villagers had small pieces of land, and added to their income by driving peats from the hills to the town. They were rather eccentric folk, and if an order was given to any of them for peats, meal, or anything else, the party who had given the order would find whatever he had ordered lying at his door in the morning, having been placed there during the night. The object of this procedure was to prevent the families in Tarbuckie knowing what each other were doing, some rivalry evidently existing among them. When they were going from home, they would start off in a contrary direction to that which they intended to take, for the purpose of leading their watchful neighbours off the scent. Among the parties who resided at Tarbuckie were George and Alexander Chalmers, two brothers, who had a good-sized farm; John Boyne, shoemaker and crofter, and his two brothers; James Forbes,crofter; Alex. Hay, shoemaker and crofter; John Sinclair, wheelwright; and David Farquhar. An individual of weakly mind, named William Michie, resided in the village, but committed an offence which made him think it advisable to quit the district. One Sunday forenoon he was left at home in charge of the "broth" while the family were at the chapel at Preshome. Taking the beef out of the pot he ate it. It seems he thought it necessary to find a substitute for the beef and seeing the cat handy he placed it in the pot. When the family came home Willie was not to be seen, but the broth was boiling on the fire, and they proceeded to take their dinners. The discovery of a great quantity of cat's hairs, however, aroused suspicion, and on examining the pot pussy was found in place of the beef. Willie never turned up to receive the scolding which he knew he deserved.

Johnnie Toll

Fully twenty years ago the death occurred of a half-witted personage known as Johnnie Toll. His right name was John Taylor. He was for many years well known about Buckie and afforded much amusement to the young folk, who were in the habit of tormenting him, a species of fun to which he seemed not to be averse, but rather encouraged. A romantic and rather improbable story is given of the manner in which his intellect became clouded, but is held to be strictly true. It is stated that Johnnie was a ploughman, and fell in love with the daughter of his employer, who returned his attachment. The girl's mother, however, was averse to the match, which she endeavoured to break off, but without result. At a "winter" or ball at the farm it is said that drink which was given to Taylor was drugged. Being with the girl he invited her also to partake, which she did, and the result was that not only did Taylor become a confirmed imbecile but his sweetheart took to bed, from which she was never able to rise. That the girl should also suffer was never intended, and was held to be a punishment on the parties who conspired against Taylor. A favourite pastime in which he indulged was planting herrings at the back of dykes in the vicinity of Nether Buckie Ha'. A standing joke of parties who were aware of Johnnie's predilections was to ask him how the herrings were growing, to which he always returned the cheerful answer that they were doing well. He had a grudge against a laird in the district, and the manner in which he showed his dislike was to demolish the laird's dykes when he was up country. He kept a shop in Buckie at one time, and it is said, to the discredit of the fishers, that they took away his goods on credit and made a point of not paying for them. The consequence was that he soon became bankrupt, but managed eventually, honest soul, to pay his creditors 20s in the pound. He had a brother who kept the Tollbar at Kittybrewster, with whom he resided for some time. He, however, tramped back to Buckie, and resumed his old trade of packman, at which he continued until he shuffled off the "mortal coil."

A Skeleton and its Teeth

An amusing incident is related in regard to the finding of a skeleton when the foundation of the present stone bridge across the Burn of Buckie was being dug. An individual had envied the beautiful teeth in the skull, and abstracted a few at a moment when he thought he was unobserved. His movements, however, had been noted by a wag, who determined to play off a joke upon him. About midnight the man in possession of the teeth was awakened from sleep by a voice in dramatic tones saying-"I want my teeth; I want my teeth." In horror the awakened sleeper gazed about, and saw what he thought an apparition vanish. Then all was quiet again. When daylight appeared a few interested and amused watchers saw the victim of the midnight apparition slip out of his house and proceed to where the bones of the defunct had been relaid, and digging up the earth reverentially returned the teeth he had possessed himself of.

Discovery of an old Gibbet: We are indebted to Mr Crammond, M.A., Cullen, for the following interesting chapter:

A reader of the old records of the Burgh of Cullen alighted the other day on the court record of the trial and execution of a man at Clunehill, Deskford, in the year 1699. The memory of such an event had entirely died away in the district, except that Mr McHattie, the farmer of Clunehill, whose mother died lately, at the age of 100 years, had once been told that a man had been hanged in the "Gallows Knowe" there. Another man, now aged nearly 90, tells of a tradition that a gibbet once stood on the Clunehill, near the old highway leading from the old town of Cullen to Keith, and that when it was being erected, a cadger, belonging to Keith, was on his way homewards with his ass, when the workmen, to test the efficiency of the gallows, seized the poor cadger and hanged him on the spot, and on dark and stormy nights 'tis said the cries of that poor ass for his lost master can still be heard in the woods around. The place is altogether "eerie and uncanny." Nearby is Pattenbringan, with a singularly complete and interesting record history of some five centuries, and in former times no one ever ventured to entertain a doubt that in the woods surrounding the remains of its ancient walls the cries of murdered bairns could be distinctly heard, especially where the elements were at their wild work. Certain at least it is, as one old man still alive can vouch, for he was one of the party - three young men, 'tween the gloamin' and the mirk, set out one night on a quiet poaching expedition. They got as far as the old house of Pattinbringan when, to their amazement, they saw on the top of a feal dyke a lady all in white. They threw their guns from their hands, and never rested until they reached their homes. The memory of that night never left them. Not far off from this same spot occurred too, a few years ago, a singular "murder," but, as neither the murderer nor the murdered party was ever discovered, it is unnecessary to rehearse the details. One result of that "murder" was that for long no fisherwoman, on her way to Deskford, would venture near the spot. In passing it may be noticed as not having been observed hitherto, that at the old house of Pattinbringan are two large stones, evidently the remains of an old burial circle. They are horneblende blocks, and therefore brought from a considerable distance to the east, and covered with markings. These markings, however, have not as yet received a careful examination, and are at present believed to be marks caused in the course of ploughing. Strange to say and this point has not been observed before, all burial circles in this district command a good view of the sea, even in cases where the circles might have been expected to be otherwise erected. In proof of this may be mentioned the circles well-know to have stood at the site of the Windmill of Glassaugh, also the circle on the farm of Towie, from which the valuable silver chain and other remains now in Banff Museum were obtained; the circle on Bankhead farm called 'Brannan's Stones, now clustered together from their original site, and containing interesting cup-markings; also the sit at Pattinbringan; also the Law Hill and other sites in the parish of Rathven, etc. Some explanation should be attempted why these circles of stones, usually called burial circles, have in this district invariably been erected so as to command a singularly good view of the sea, even when the opposite would in some cases much more naturally have been expected. That the Norsemen were always buried in sight of their beloved sea is well known.

The reader above referred to examined the "Gallows Knowe" and found a slight heap of stones almost covered with earth which was a similar mound of less extent. He suggested, to a party present, that underneath that heap of stones was certain to be found the bones of the man who was hanged, as such persons could not be buried within a churchyard. A slight examination was accordingly made, and in the one mound was found the remains of the gibbet, and in the other the remains of the man who was hanged. In the former case were two flat circular stones of about two feet in diameter superimposed and surrounded by some half-a-dozen longitudinal stones fixed perpendicularly in the ground for the purpose of keeping the tree resting on the flat stones rigid. The gibbet was evidently, therefore, a single tree. It was placed in such a position as to command a good view of the old town of Cullen, and was, no doubt, valuable to the burghers as preventing them from indulging in the vagaries to which they were at times somewhat liable. Still the Royal Burgh was able to boast of a gallows of its own, part of the woodwork of which stood till within the memory of a townsman who died not many years ago at the age of upwards of eighty years. That a gallows existed on the Clunehill long before the period referred to is, however, evident (it was in the year 1616 the Regality of Ogilvie was constituted), for it is recorded in the Register of Horning's in the Sheriff Clerk's Office, Banff, that in the year 1646 the laird of Glassaugh came to the house of Patrick Gelly, notary public in Fordyce, along with the laird's brother and two servants armed with weapons, and provided with "fire and kindled peats, of plain purpose to burn the complainer's house and haill family" (the said complainer, Patrick Gelly, was the laird's brother-in -law), and because Patrick Gelly would not deliver up a discharge for a debt, the party "bodden with their weapons by way of hamessacken maist presumptuoslie and cruellie put violent hands on the person of the said Patrick Gelly, took him captive, and prisoner to the Cleanehill of Deskfuird," etc., evidently to terrify him by threat of the gallows that stood there, and it did not require the cuteness of a notary to be aware that probably never in this district were violence and murder more rampant than at that time. However, after being captive for several days during which he was carried over the hills to Enzie, he lived to bring his case before the Sheriff. In the "back years" of King William, law again asserted itself, and never was hanging in this district more common than towards the close of the seventeenth century.

"The Sherref heirby decerns and adjudges you, the said James Gray, to be takin upon Fryday nixt, the sevinteint day of this instant moneth, above sett downe from the prison of Cullen, wher you now remaine to the Clune Hill thereoff and gibitt standing thereon betwixt the hours of two and four o'clock in the afternoon, and thereupon hang'd up by the neck by the hand of the common executioner till ye be dead. As also decernes and adjudges you, the said John Gray, the said day and place to be whipt about the said gibbit and your ear nailed thereto by the said executioner, and to be banished from the shyre in all tyme comein heirafter for ever under the pain of immediate death if he shall happin to be againe found or apprehended therin without any furder sentence to be pronounced against you for that effect, and ordaines your haill moveables to be exhest and inbrought and this for doome."

"NICOLAS DUNBAR."

The body was found at the depth of only eighteen inches from below the surface. It lay north to south, the head to the south. The leg and arm bones were in a fair state of preservation; the rest was almost completely decayed except that the skull was fairly well preserved. It was evident no coffin had been used. Three large stones had been placed at the head, one at the top and one at each side extremely close to the head. The bones were reverently collected and enclosed in a small chamber of rough stones. The whole was then covered with earth and a cairn of stones placed on the summit, and above this a few green branches in memoriam. The flat stone on the site of the gibbet was at a depth of about three feet. This was also restored to the same position except that it was brought nearer the surface. The stones that surrounded it were then carefully placed as before, and an old wooden roller inserted perpendicularly to mark the exact spot until a more suitable memorial be erected. The matter caused a good deal of talk in the district, as no one had the slightest idea that a body had been buried there. The tall spruce fir trees around it are only seventy years of age, and were planted in place of the old Scotch fir trees that formerly stood there until they were blown down one stormy night.

To-Names in Banffshire and Aberdeenshire a Century ago

Such names are at the present day a characteristic feature in most fishing villages, and they appear from contemporary documents to have been as much in vogue in many fishing villages so early, at least, as 1792. That they were in use much earlier on the borders is well known; e.g., Sir Richard Maitland, in his poem "Aganis the Theivis of Liddisdail," says:-

> Thai theifs that steills and tursis hame,
> Ilk ane of thame has ane to-name-
> Will of the Lawis,
> Hab of the Schawis; to mak bare wa's
> They think nae shame

Place of residence or personal peculiarities in these cases usually originated the to-name. In Banffshire in early times the to-name was frequently of a very affectionate or complimentary character, but about a generation ago it was often of such a character that there was a greater probability of keeping the peace by using it in the absence of the party referred to. The following names occur in a collection of accounts for lobsters and yellow "hadys," sold in 1792, that the writer had occasion to examine lately. In Buckie we find Peter Reid 'Old Hankam,' Wm. Reid 'Young Hankam,' John Geddes 'Kokans,' Alex. Cowie 'Sannicky,' Geo. Murray 'Costy,' Wm. Cowie 'Codlen,' Jas. Murray 'Doty,' Geo. Cowie 'Young Dozay,' Jn. Geddes 'Soger,' Jn. Geddes 'Boyn,' Jn. Geddes ' Bo.' In Portessie:- John Smith 'Laittan.' In Inverallochy:- Andrew Duthie 'Brownie,' Alex. Duthie 'Roie,' John Mason 'Brodland,' Jn. Buchan 'Lowie,' Wm. Buchan 'Sangster,' Js. Duthie 'Captain,' Andw. Duthie 'Skipper,' William Symers 'Wyltie,' Wm. Symers 'Duckie,' Js. Duthie 'Sailor,' Wm. Mey 'Patle,' Andrew Duthie 'Deally,' Wm. Steven 'Rossie.' In Cairnbulg:- And. Duthie 'Rymer,' Andrew Duthie 'Jamaica,' Js. Mey 'Cairnie,' Andw. Steven 'Dumbie,' Andw. Whyte 'Doctor,' John Steven 'Spolie,' John Duthie 'Little Jockie,' Andw. Whyte 'Buly Pope,' George Buchan 'Youl.' In Broadsea:- Gilbert Noble 'Coomby,' Geo. Crawford 'Miries,' Wm. Noble 'Waldie,' John Watt 'Todgie,' Gilbert Noble 'Cripple,' John Noble 'Ben's Son,' Andw. Noble 'Benjie,' Wm. Noble 'Bods,' Andw. Noble 'Juno,' Andw. Noble 'Young

Pownie,' Andw. Taylor 'Bouf,' Alex. Noble 'Dod,' Andw. Watt 'Todd,' Andw. Noble 'Pownie,'
Geo. Crawford 'Walgon,' Alex. Noble 'Short,' Alex. Noble 'Shankie,' W. Noble 'Bods,' etc.
Several of these to-names have continued to the present day.

A Specimen of the "Good Old Times" in Banffshire

In the year 1628 James Ogilvie of Acheries was killed in the streets of Banff. His
relict, his daughter, and his brother, together with John Gordon, the laird of Buckie, and
William Gordon, the laird of Cairnfield, his brothers uterine, and his remaining kin and
friends, complained before the court upon Sir George Ogilvie of Banff, provost of Banff, Sir
George Ogilvie of Carnousie, Robert Ogilvie, burgess of Banff, William Ogilvie, Robert
Stuart, James Anderson, Patrick Weyness, John Ross, and others, in the following terms:- Sir
George Ogilvie of Banff having a deadly hatred to James Ogilvie of Acheries, accompanied
with the said William Ogilvie, George Braibner alias "Joukie," and several others, with
swords, dirks, steelbonnets, hackbuts, daggers, pistolets, long guns, etc., contrary to the Act
of Parliament, came under silence and cloud of night by way of hamesucken about midnight
to Margaret Ogilvie her house (relict of the above James Ogilvie) in Paddocklaw, where she
and her family were in quiet and sober manner for the time in their beds taking the night's
rest, thinking to have rested in peace and security under God and our protection. Her
husband being absent and the said laird of Banff falsely usurping upon him the name of John
Gordon of Buckie, brother uterine to her said late husband, chopped at the door and under
the usurped name foresaid desired entry, and how soon she heard of the said John Gordon
his name whom she thought had been attending, at the word she rose out of her bed and
opened the door, but howsoon the laird of Banff with his associates had gotten entry they,
in a great rage and fury drew their swords and bended their pistolets, and held the points of
their swords and pistolets to her poor naked armless servants' breasts, threatening them with
present death if they revealed not where the said umquhile James was; thereafter went
athort the haill house and chambers within the same, scorched with their swords all the beds
they found within, and were resolved on set purpose to have slain and murdered her late
husband in his bed if he had been apprehended, and at that time she the said Margaret was
great with child. On the third October last the said umquhile James being directed by the
Lady Boyne for production of a sasine for removing some tenants off her liferent lands
before the Sheriff of Banff, being the Head Michaelmass Court day, the said George Ogilvie
of Banff, knight baronet and provost of the said town of Banff, and the said Sir George
Ogilvie of Carnowsie being at the said Head Court, the court being fenced and suits called
and not regarding the said place of justice at such ane solemn time the said umquhile James
Ogilvie making due court and reverence to the said Lairds of Carnowsie and Banff saluting
them, the said Laird of Banff of precogitate malice and evil will conceived to him against the
said James Ogilvie, perceiving his head uncovered and his bonnet off, struck the said
umquhile James on the bare head with a batton to the effusion of his blood in great quantity
and thereafter the said Lairds of Banff and Carnowsie and the haill remanent persons
complained upon, drew their swords within the said tolbooth in time of court, and "strake
most fearclie and crewlie" at the said James who, defending himself with his sword, escaped
furth of the said tolbooth of Banff to the King's high causeway of Banff. They most fiercely
pursued and followed the said James Ogilvie, "alangouslie the calsay off the said burghe be
the space of tua buttis and mair," and having overtaken him, and he being alone, and they
above twenty persons, most barbarously, cruelly, and unhumanly anew beset the said James,
on every side being a naked man, destitute of all and armour and help, except only a sword
in his hand, and there most cruelly, shamefully and unmercifully murdered the said James
and gave him many cruel and deadly strokes upon his head and divers other parts of his body,

and, especially, the said Laird of Banff with his own hand struck the said James behind his back with a sword through the fifth rib and through the liver, being "ane dead straike," and also the said Laird of Carnowsie most barbarously, shamefully, unhumanly shot the said unquhie James Ogilvie with a pistol charged with two bullets, the top of his thigh being broken ...[Rest Lost.]

Three years afterwards (April 15, 1631, that is a few weeks after John Philip was burned at Banff for witchcraft) the minister of Boyndie summoned Sir George Ogilvie of Banff, charging him to compear and satisfy for the "slauchter" of Jas. Ogilvie, but he compeared not

CHAPTER VII

The history of the Church of Rathven

With Rathven the parish of Bellie was in former days conjoined, and in this district there has existed from the days of the Reformation downwards a colony of Roman Catholics, as well as a colony of Episcopalians. Rathven was for long the anchor of the Roman Catholic Church in Scotland, and has sent forth from one-third to one-fourth of all the Vicars-Apostolic in this country, besides a long array of priests and literary men. To the influence of the Earls of Huntly is to be traced the vigour of the Roman cause in this the land of the Gordons.

The earliest reference to the Church of Rathven is in the deed establishing the hospital of Rathven (1224-1226) when John Bisset gave to God and the Church of St. Peter of Rothfan the patronage of the Kirk of Kyltalargy for sustaining seven leprous persons in the said hospital. In 1334 Thomas Hay of Urchny founded a chaplainry in the Church of Rathven with five merks yearly rental, for the weal of the soul of the founder and his wife, and of Christian Crukschank and others the chaplain to serve at the altar of Our Lady in the Church of Rathven, and to receive a payment of five merks yearly from the lands of Urchny, in the county of Nairn. In 1445 when the number of Canons in the Cathedral of Aberdeen was increased from twelve, one of the new stalls was bestowed on Rathven by Bishop Lindsay with a salary of 80 pounds. The presentation to the Prebend of Rathven rested alternately with the Bishop of Aberdeen and the Archbishop of St. Andrews. Rathven contributed £4 2s 6d towards the expenses (£2500) of the Representatives sent to the Council of Trent.

By 1483 the churches of Rathven and Farskane were annexed. Between 1519 and 1531 John Friscobaldi, rector of Rothwan, is recorded as giving to the high altar of St. Machar's Cathedral at Aberdeen a pall of cloth of gold, having the arms of Florence embroidered on it.

At the Reformation the parson of Rathven was George Hay, one of the Rannes family, who sided with the Reformers, but there is little evidence that his conduct in this respect met with the general approval of his parishioners. In 1565 Mr Hay was commissioned by the General Assembly to visit kirks, schools, and colleges, from Dee to Spey, to eradicate Popery. In 1570 he was elected Moderator of the General Assembly. He appears to have been the same George Hay who wrote the confutation of the Abbot of Crossraguell's Mass (Fasti). He died in 1588.

At the re-establishment of Episcopacy in 1610, the minister of Rathven was James Lyll or Lyle. Bellie seems to have been separated from the charge in 1590, and the parsonage and vicarage of Dundurcus in 1605. The Books of Assignations show James Lyll, minister of "Rothven, Forsken, Dundurcus" in 1590, and of "Rathven, Forsken" in 1607.

About 1620 the kirk lands of Rannes, Connage, Wester Freuchnie, Nether Freuchnie, 24 acres of Rathven, with tower , etc., in the barony of Rothven were let to Mr James Hay for £35 7s 2d.

Mr Lyll was succeeded in 1620 by David Forrester, who was translated from North Leith to which he was re-translated in 1627. He is said to have been earnest in proceeding against Papists. The Presbytery minutes inform us that on August 24, 1624, there was a visitation of the Kirk of Rathven, when there were present ane reverend father in God, Patrick, Bishop of Aberdeen; elders - The Goodman of Buckie, younger; James Hay, of

Rannes; John Ogilvie, of Glassaugh; Andrew Stewart, of Tannachie; Patrick Stewart, in Farnauchtie; William Gordon of Farnaughtie; John Gordoune, of Nether Buckie; John Stewart, in Over Buckie, etc "The minister is appointed on Sunday afternoon to convene one or two towns for catechising. As concerning the collection of the alms, finds the order good, as also that the penalties and burial silver is formally and exactly collected ..... Inquisition being made how the Sabbath Day was kept by all sorts of persons it was found by the declaration of the minister and elders that the same was better kept than before. The act against charmers, diviners, and seekers of responses ratified."

In the minute of Presbytery, August 9, 1626, it is stated that Mr. Forrester declared of a horrible and fearful desolation in Rathven, and specially that George Gordoun of Farnauchtie proclaimed publicly on the last Sabbath immediately after the sermon at the kirk style in the name and authority of the Marquis of Huntly, that non within the Marquis's bounds should frequent the hearing of the Word on the Sabbath Day at the Kirk of Rathven, under pain of losing house and land, and under pain of incurring the wrath of the said Marquis, their master.

Mr Forrester was succeeded in 1627 by Mr John Logie, who was translated from Bethelny. Mr Logie was deposed in 1647 for his intercourse with the Marquis of Huntly, but reponed by the Assembly in the following year, and "socht" by the parish of Keith in 1649. He died prior to the restoration of Episcopacy in 1661, and Parliament granted £50 to his children out of the vacant stipends on account of his sufferings. After the deposition of Mr Logie in 1647 for companying with "excommunicated Papists and open rebels," Mr Patrick Glass was presented to the charge by George Hay of Rannes, but the Presbytery refused to institute, finding that the presentation and manner of purchasing it did militate against the Acts of the General Assembly.

In the minute of August 17, 1630, "the minister regretted that his Session was not so frequent in meeting and in executing the acts, specially fishers and mills working and grinding on the Sabbath."

On June 2, 1647, George Gordoun in Leitchestoune, Andrew Stewart of Tannachie, Alex. Gourdone in Oxhill, Johne Harper in Cowhorach, Robert Stewart, George Gordoune (son to William Gordoune of Thornibank), all in the parish of Rathven, compeared before the Presbytery in humble manner on their knees, confessing their grief and sorrow for going on in the wicked rebellion, being accessorie to the great effusion of blood in this kingdom against the work of Reformation. They were directed back to satisfy their own parish kirk in sackcloth.

On the 16th of June Mr John Watsone reported that he had gone to Rathven on the 6th of June and intimated the deposition of Mr John Logie, and declared the kirk vacant, which the said John Logie, being present, did homologate, confessing himself to be justly deposed. He also intimated that the parties named in the minute of June 2 had sat in humble manner in their prescribed habits all the time of the lecture and sermon, and afterwards acknowledged their great offences on their knees, and with uplifted hands promised to detest and abhor all such courses in time coming, and to stand to the work of Reformation. He had also cited John Gordone in Gollachie, William Gordoune in Buckie, and John Gordon, son to Thomas Gordoune in Clashtirim, to compear before the Commissioners of the Kirk at Edinburgh on the second Wednesday of July.

There appeared before the Presbytery William Gordoune in Cairnfielde, James Gordon in Beldornie, Adam Gordon, in Soccothe, and James Gordon in Cowhorauche, who on their knees confessed having gone on in the wicked rebellion, and made ample promises of good behaviour in the future. They were ordained to make repentance in the Kirk of Fordyce, as Rathven was vacant.

On February 24, 1648, the Presbytery, considering that the towns and lands of Forskane, Brunton, Castelfield, Muldavat, Patinbroynaud were nearer to Cullen than Rathven, annexed them to the Kirk of Cullen.

In 1649 Mr William Scrogie, A.M., son of Dr. Alex. Scrogie, of Old Machar, was appointed minister of Rathven, and continued in charge of the parish till 1668. Mr. Scrogie declined a call to Aberdeen in 1664. He was rector of King's College, Aberdeen, from 1663 to 1666, when he was appointed Bishop of Argyll. On his settlement in Rathven the manse was in a deplorable state of dilapidation, as the following minute shows:- (1) A stonne hous sklaitted wtout rigging stone; (2) in the hall a double firre dorre, three windowes wt. old broads of timber, whereof one is glassed wanting some lozens, in the end of the hall is a pantrie wt. a thinne wall of stak and rys, wt. a single dor; (3) the passage up to the loft hath ane old single broken firre dor and a timber stair; (4) above the wtter chalmer bath two windowes wanting glass wt. old broads of timber, a partitione wall of old single dealls, wtin qlk is a chalmer fylled above wt. ellewen dealls. In it ar two windowes qroff one hath some broken glass in it. In the studie a glassen window wt, sindrie broken lozens, but well broaded. On the wast side of the closs a barne wt. a for and back dor, a byr wanting a dor, and ane stable wt. a broken dor, all wch houses are ruinous. On the east syd a barne wt. two dors, a garden wt. dykes wtout the gat, upon the north syd thereoff is ane little old kill.

In 1653 there was no meeting of the Presbytery on the 22nd February, "be reasoune that the moderator, Mr William Scrogie, had advertised the brethren that his bedfellow was departed this lyff, and she was to be buried that day."

Bishop Scrogie was succeeded in the charge of Rathven in 1669 by Mr John Hay, one of the Rannes family, on the "supplications of Mr Jhon Hay, tutor of Ranesse; Mr Andrew Hay of Kairnefield; George Gordon of Thorniebank; William Ord of Findochty. Mr Hay was deprived by the Privy Council in 1689 for not reading the Proclamation of the Estates, and for not praying for William and Mary as enjoined. In 1694 he was deposed. From the account of a visitation in 1688 we learn that Mr Hay had "a good testimonie from his veri adversaries. He preached twice every Lord's Day in summer and once in winter, and was cairful in reproving sin and preventing apostasie to poprie. He did administer the Sacrament of the Lord's Supper every year at Easter and some years at Pentecost, He was a pattern of piety, justice, temperance, etc." So firm a hold had Mr Hay on the affections of his parishioners that it was with great difficulty, and only after a long and arduous struggle, that the Presbyterians were able to supplant him after the Revolution of 1688 and the consequent disestablishment of Episcopacy.

When the crash of the Revolution came it was greatly in favour of Episcopacy in the parish that the Church of Rathven was served by a pastor so able, diligent, and faithful as Mr John Hay. The difference between the Epicopalians and Presbyterians was exceedingly small. The Holy Eucharist was, with occasional exceptions, celebrated only once a year. The surplice was not worn, even at the celebration of the Holy Eucharist, till nearly a century and a half later; and probably the only liturgical formulary in use was the English Ordinal. The result of the attempt to conciliate Presbyterians by minimising the difference between them and the Episcopal Church proved a miserable failure. After the deposition of Mr Hay in 1694 the Presbytery in their minutes complained of the supine negligence and utter unwillingness of the parish to call a Presbyterian minister. The course adopted by the heritors and elders of Rathven seems to have been to comply so far with the requests of the Presbytery as to make a presentation to the charge, taking care, however, to present one agreeable to their own way of thinking, and therefore objectionable to the Presbytery. Then when the Presbytery declined to institute, and proceeded to nominate a man after their own mind, matters were so arranged that the right of presentation speedily returned to the heritors and elders. This opposition to Presbyterianism seemed not to be the act of a few individuals, but of the whole parish, for when a Mr Wm. Mitchell went to Rathven to preach he got neither access nor auditors. A "Mr Murray was the second day at Rathven, but got no access, and the third day he was at Rathven, where he got patent doors but no auditors, not so much as one to ring a bell, but many of the people went to the late incumbent's who is suspected to be the present author of all their disorders." This game of see-saw between the heritors of Rathven and the Presbytery of Fordyce went on (with an appeal by the Presbytery in 1698 to the Earl of Findlater and Castelfield, Sheriff-Depute of Banff, to put the laws in execution against Sabbath-breaking and not attending ordinances) until August, 1699, when the Presbytery gave a call to Mr William Chalmer, minister of Gartly, "in regard to his great skill and insight in all polemical divinity, especially the papist controversies, his great talent of preaching, and circumspect conversation." On the 20th April, 1700, we are informed, a fast was "observed by the congregation of Rathven previous to Mr Chalmer's admission." On April 24th Mr Chalmer was "admitted," but his admittance was not of a very hearty description. The Presbytery met in James Coull's house in the Kirktoun of Rathven, as the heritors refused them access to the church. The church officer was called for but could not be found. The heritors gave in "a paper to the Presbytery signed by George Gordon of Buckie, William Ord of Findauchtie, John Gordon of Daviestown, George Gordon of Arradoul, Patrick Stuart of Tannachie, etc." The Presbytery found the paper inconsistent with the heritors' former obligation, and the objections irrelevant. The Moderator being again denied access to the church, preached and admitted Mr Chalmer in the churchyard, some men and women scolding and railing against the Presbytery and Mr Chalmer the while. In the afternoon the Presbytery met at Cullen to consider Mr Chalmer 'having been abused and his person at hazard at Rathven upon Sabbath last by a rabble which had fallen upon him, offered violence to his person, pulling from him his hat, cloak, and gloves, blacking and scratching his face, stoning him with stones, so as he had not access to the church but was forced to preach in James Coull's house. The rabble to be represented to authority. On July 10th of the same year, "the Presbytery, being informed that Mr Geo. Hay, son to the deceased Major Hay of Rannochie, keeps a meeting house in the parish of Rathven, did appoint the Moderator to employ a messenger-at-arms for summoning him before the Presbytery." Although instituted in April, it was not till the following August that Mr Chalmer gained access to the church of Rathven, after the matter had been referred by the Presbytery to the Sheriff-Depute of Banff, and to the Commission or the General Assembly. On 14th March, 1704, a visitation of Rathven was held by the Presbytery, but notwithstanding Mr Chalmer had been settled in the parish for four years, and had civil powers at his back, "none of the heritors compeared, and but very few of the people." He complained that a meeting-house was kept up, to which a great number of the people resorted. Rathven must have been a very uncongenial abode to him, and it is not surprising that he removed to King Edward in August, 1704.

After Mr Chalmer's removal, the Presbytery were unable to get a successor appointed to him, the heritors and people of Rathven being "peremptorily resolved to adhere to Mr Hay." In the beginning of 1709, Mr John Hay, clergyman, and Mr Alex. Smith, schoolmaster at Rathven, were cited before the Presbytery. Mr Hay was indisposed and did not appear, but several of the heritors presented an address, desiring the Presbytery, taking into consideration the peculiar circumstances of the parish, would desist from further prosecution of Mr Hay. The Presbytery declined to accede to the request. Mr Smith appeared before the Presbytery, "and was required to subscribe the Confession of Faith, but he answered that being a young man he had not yet sufficiently considered the same, and therefore desired that some time might be allowed him, which the Presbytery granted." Mr Smith's study of the Confession of Faith does not seem to have impressed him in its favour, for under entry June 19th, 1711, we read - "Smith intruder at Rathven. The Presbytery being informed that one Mr Smith, schoolmaster in Rathven hath lately set up a meeting-house there contrary to the law and order, do therefore appoint to cause summon him to their next time." The summons was duly executed, but Mr Smith did not appear, and the Presbytery appointed two of their number "to address the Justices of Peace in order to the removing of the said Mr Smith from Rathven." At a subsequent meeting the Presbytery are told that 'Mr Smith is about to move of his own accord; and a month later, the two appointed to look after the matter report "that they did address one of the Justices of the Peace for removing Mr Smith, intruder in Raffan, who gave it as his opinion that the said Mr Smith should be summoned at their next quarterly meeting at Banff. He is summoned accordingly."

The decease of Mr John Hay in 1711 appears to have been considered by the Presbytery a suitable opportunity for renewing their efforts to get a Presbyterian minister at Rathven; but the heritors and heads of families were still obdurate, and the Presbytery was about to make an appointment when the Patronage Act of Queen Anne was passed. This Act seemed to tie the hands of the Presbytery, and no nomination was made until after the Synod was consulted. Various members of the Presbytery were appointed to give supply at Rathven, but on their arrival there they invariably found the church doors locked, and no congregation. On one occasion one of their number, Mr Irvine, took the Sheriff-Depute along with him and demanded the keys of the church door from the beadle. The beadle replied that he had given them to the Laird of Rannas, who had called for them on the previous day, whereupon he was sent by the Sheriff to demand them from the Laird. But the beadle was in no haste to return, and meanwhile the Episcopal clergyman, Mr George Hay, arrived on the scene, accompanied by the Marchioness of Huntly, and entering the church took possession of the pulpit, and so Mr Irvine was obliged to return without having accomplished his object. The charge was offered to a Mr John Forbes, and then to a Mr Walter Sim, but both declined. In August, 1714, Lord Deskford twice urged the Presbytery to delay making an appointment, but evidently little heed was paid, for on the 24th a call was again given to Mr Sim. He, however, found an excuse for declining the second offer, having received a call to be minister of Glass. It was then resolved to give a call to Mr Robert Gordon. At a meeting of the Presbytery on November 23, 1714, there compeared the Lairds of Rannas, Mildaviot, and Oxhill, craving that the Presbytery would consider the particular circumstances of the parish of Rathven, and allow Mr George Hay to continue there in the exercise of his ministry, alleging that none other could be useful there and that if the Presbytery should proceed to call and ordain any other man among them, the generalitie of the parishioners would apostasise to Poperie. The Presbytery refused the petition, Mr George Hay being of the Episcopal Communion, and having intruded into that church contrare to law. The Laird of Rannas took instruments, and protested, as the presentation was not fallen onto the hands of the Presbytery. The Presbytery reply that the right was fallen into their hands about eight years ago." The apostasising to Popery was no empty threat, for six years later we find the Presbytery taking into serious consideration "the growth of Popery in the parish of Rathven," and in the Representation made by the General Assembly in 1722 "to his Majesty anent the growth of Popery," it is stated that "in the parish of Raffan there are nearly 800 Papists, the greatest part of whom have been perverted of late years. In 1780, according to the report made to Propaganda, the Roman Catholics had 1150 communicants in the Rathven district.

After the Presbytery had in vain offered the living to several, the call was at last accepted by Mr Robert Gordon in the end of 1714. The Presbytery met at Banff on December 28th of that year, when "Mr Gordon delivered his exegesis and exercise. The Lairds of Ranas and Mildaviot, together with a great many of the parishioners and inhabitants of the parish of Rathven, having stayed in the churchyard all the time of the exercise, sent word to the Presbytery craving access, which was allowed, and they gave in a petition, subscribed by a great many persons, in favour of Mr George Hay, and pleading that the Presbytery would delay Mr Gordon's ordination, and connive at the said Mr Hay's possession of the Church and Manse of Rathven till the ensuing General Assembly, before which they said they would represent the singular circumstances of their parish, and did not doubt of getting a favourable return. The Presbytery refuse the petition. The Laird of Ranas appeals to the General Assembly, whereupon the gentlemen and parishioners went their way, and a great many of them threatened the Presbytery if they should proceed to ordain Mr Gordon minister of Rathven, and impudently crying out that the Presbytery, if they would come to Rathven to ordain Mr Gordon, might bring his coffin and winding sheets with them, upon which threatening language instruments were being taken in the hands of Thomas Murray, N.P., when some of the said parishioners laid hands upon the said Thomas Murray, and violently hailed him away."

Immediately after this, criminal letters were presented against Mr George Hay, because he "absolutely refused to leave off his intrusion, or come under any obligation to forbear preaching." This seems to have further exasperated the parishioners, for they no longer restricted themselves to passive resistance when the members of the Presbytery attempted to officiate in the church. Thus we read that on January 23rd, 1715, Mr Irvin, "according to the appointment of the Presbytery, went in order to have supplied the Church of Rathven, but that when he was coming near to the church he was met by a great company of women who desired him to go back, otherwise he might come to smart for it, and he, offering to go forward, they laid hold on his horse bridle, struck him in the face, throwing a great many stones at himself to the effusion of his blood, and that he escaped with danger of his life. Mr Ross, another member of the Presbytery, prudent man! went to the bounds according to the Presbytery's appointment, but hearing of Mr Irvin's treatment turned back.

At a meeting of the Presbytery at Banff on March 17, 1715, there "compeared of the Lairds of Ranas, Buckie, Mildaviot, and Oxhill, with a great many of the parishioners of Rathven, and gave in an unsubscribed paper, which they alleged contained objections against Mr Gordon's ordination, which, though it was stuffed with a great many impertinent queries about and reflections upon Presbyterian government, did not contain any material objection against the life and doctrine of Mr Gordon. The said gentleman also said that Mr Gordon had in some companies called them fools and beasts, and advanced that he should be minister of Rathven over their bellies, which he peremptorily refused, and protested. After protesting, the gentlemen removed, the multitude of parishioners attending them venting themselves, after a most insolent and extravagant manner, in threatenings, curses, and horrid imprecations against the Presbytery and Mr Gordon, after such a tumultuary manner as the Presbytery had ground to fear violence from them, whereupon they were obliged immediately to get out of the church."

On March 28 the Presbytery decided not to ordain Mr Gordon in the Church of Cullen for fear of violence, but to ordain him in the Church of Boyndie, thus placing 15 miles between them and the discontented parishioners of Rathven. Mr Gordon was accordingly ordained at Boyndie on March 27, 1715.

Mr George Hay was summoned to appear before the Lords of Justiciary at Aberdeen on 10th May. A compromise was, however, effected by Mr Hay giving his bond, before the Lords of Justiciary that he would "remove out of the Manse betwixt the Lambmass next, under the failzie of £50 sterling, for which Charles Hay of Ranas and John Hay of Logie were cautioners, whereupon the King's Advocate Depute deserted the diet against Mr Hay and the rabblers of Mr Irvine." At the same time, Mr Robert Gordon obtained an 'Act of Adjournal' from the Lords of Justiciary, appointing the Earl of Findlater, Sheriff-Prinipal of Banffshire, and his deputies to give peaceable possession of the Church of Rathven to him. On the Act being presented to the Sheriff, he gave instructions to Provost Mark, one of his deputies, to take the necessary steps to have it enforced. The deputy, accompanied by "a considerable company, both of gentry and commons in arms," went with Mr Gordon to the Church of Rathven. On their way they were met by a vast number of the inhabitants of the parish, both men and women, who sought to stop their progress by throwing stones, "cursing and imprecating horridly," etc. After fighting their way through the crowd, the Sheriff-Depute and his company at last, with great hazard and difficulty, reached the church doors, only to find them barricaded. The doors were ultimately broken open, whereupon Mr Gordon preached his first sermon in the church, the parishioners remaining outside and giving expression to their displeasure. Thus, after a contest of eleven years, did the Presbyterians a second time oust the Episcopalians from the Church of Rathven. With the exception of the four years, from 1700 to 1704, of Mr Chalmer's unsuccessful ministry, they had been unable to place one of their ministers in the parish for the first 27 years after the Revolution. Even in 1722 we read - "The Presbytery can with difficulty supply Rathven, most of the members being so circumstanciate with Jacobite meeting-houses within or upon the confines of the parish that they cannot leave their people for one Lord's day."

By the advice of the ministers of Aberdeen Mr Gordon went in the summer of 1715 to Edinburgh to represent the circumstances of Rathven to the Justice General. Most of the heritors and a great number of the common people of Rathven took part in the rising of 1715, and Mr Gordon, on his return from Edinburgh, afraid that he would not be safe within the bounds of his own Presbytery, took refuge in Moray, from whence he returned next spring to his own parish. In 1718 we find him complaining to the Presbytery that, notwithstanding all his toil and efforts he cannot get the people to attend his ministration; and saying that but for the support of a handful, he would sink under his load of difficulties and disappointments. Doubtless the strain told upon his health, for in November, 1720, he died.

Mr Gordon was succeeded by Mr Andrew Ker, who was translated in 1723 from Kirkwall Second Charge, being called by the Presbytery jure devoluts with correspondents. In July, 1724, the summer after his appointment, he represented to the Presbytery that one Mr William Longmuir, lately ordained deacon by Bishop Badderar, was officiating in the parish of Rathven, and did not pray for His Majesty King George, and that unless immediate steps were taken for Mr Longmuir's removal, he was afraid he would break up his congregation. The Presbytery were of the opinion that in such cases application should be made by the minister of the parish to the proper judge, and that if redress be not obtained by this means, then the Presbytery would support him in taking such other steps as might be found necessary. Accordingly the matter was brought under the notice of the Earl of Findlater, Sheriff of Banffshire, and his lordship promised to interpose his authority to get Mr Longmuir removed from the parish of Rathven. But lest the Sheriff should show any remissness in dealing with the case, Mr Ker was appointed by the Presbytery "to keep him in mind of it." As Mr Longmuir lived on the estate of Rannes the Earl deferred doing anything until he should first write the Laird. Very likely a friendly hint of the danger which threatened him was given by the Laird of Rannes to Mr Longmuir, for the latter opportunely became indisposed and removed from the parish for a time, so that nothing more could be done in the matter "until it be known whether he gives further diversion to the people from ordinances or not." Mr Longmuir did not absent himself for any length of time, for two months later Mr Ker reported that Mr Lomgmuir had returned to the Laird of Rannes' estate. The Presbytery then appointed Messrs Irvine and Lawtie to wait upon the Laird and use their influence with him in order to Mr Longmuir being removed from the parish. As no satisfactory reply could be got from the Laird, the Presbytery resolved to renew their application to the Sheriff-Principal. Meanwhile, however, a fresh cause of offence was given by Mr Longmuir administering the sacrament to "a multitude of whom he could have no manner of knowledge, never having been in that country before, and amongst them several persons who had only deserted Mr Ker's ministry for two or three Sabbaths before, and besides, many of them known to be common and customary swearers and Sabbath breakers." The Presbytery agreed to represent the matter to the Assembly, but the result is not told. Possibly Mr Ker had enough to do to attend to his own affairs without prosecuting Episcopalians or Roman Catholics. It appears that he had entered into a simoniacal contract in order to obtain the appointment to Rathven. His security for carrying out this contract was James Ogilvy, sometime collector of Excise at Aberdeen. After Mr Ogilvie's decease, his widow, Lady Glengairack, summoned Mr Ker before the Lords of Council and Session, in order to be released from the obligation undertaken by her late husband. At first the Presbytery gave their support to Mr Ker, and resolved to carry on a process of calumny against Lady Glengairack for having charged Mr Ker with "what evidently implied at least an appearance of simony." Five months later, however, the following entry was made in their minutes:- "Anent Mr Ker's affair the Presbytery doe judge that the said Mr Ker, his conduct has been rash, weak, imprudent, and uncircumspect, and truly blameworthy, and that he has been too active in procuring the said settlement, and, therefore, though such a behaviour deserves censure, yet, considering the lamentable circumstances of his parish, and the great probability of his being rendered unuseful and his parish left as a prey to the common enemy, had the same been inflicted in a more public manner, do appoint their Moderator to rebuke him sharply, and exhort and admonish him to more prudence and circumspection in time comeing, which accordingly was done."

Mr Ker died in 1751. After his death William Gordon of Shellagreen appeared before the Presbytery and gave in a disposition from Lady Rannes, investing him with the patronage of the Church of Rathven. The Presbytery objected that no title was provided from the late Charles Hay to her ladyship. Shellagreen stated that in the present circumstances of the family of Rannes [the Laird had been out in the '45, and many thrilling stories are still told in the district of his numerous hairbreadth escapes] the production of Rannes disposition to his Lady might, in some events, be very inconvenient to that family. "There was given in a petition from several of the Episcopal persuasion in the parish of Rathven, promising that, if Mr Grant was settled amongst them, then they would submit to his ministry, and hoping the Presbytery would proceed to his settlement. Afterwards Mr Gordon produced the disposition, and the Presbytery proceeded to the settlement of Mr Grant as required.

George Donaldson was the next minister of the parish, his term of office being from 1791 to 1821. He was settled at Rathven on September 22, 1791, but not in a very pleasant manner, as the following minute shows: "The kirk officer having made the usual intimation at the most patent door of the church, Wm. Taylor, an unmarried man in Buckie, gave in what he called 'a petition to the ministers of the Gospel of the Presbytery of Fordyce,' as he said, by a number of Protestant parishioners. The Presbytery found the same irrelevant and informal. The Presbytery then resolved to proceed to the admission of Mr Donaldson, upon which the said Wm. Taylor protested and appealed to the Synod of Aberdeen. After this, the Presbytery ordered the officer to ring the bell, that they might proceed to the admission of Mr Donaldson in the Church of Rathven. The officer having returned to the schoolhouse, where the Presbytery met, reported that a mob had got into the church, and barricaded all the doors, particularly the door leading to the bell. The Presbytery, together with Mr Donaldson, in company with several of the heritors, proceeded to the church doors, and found the circumstances of the case as the officer had reported. After having tried all pacifying measures with the people, they found that they would not give them access. They also found a tumultuous mob assembled in the church to keep fast the doors. In these circumstances, and to avoid more disagreeable circumstances from the mob, who seemed to be unaccountably exasperated, the Presbytery agreed to adjourn to the nearest Parish Church, the Church of Cullen, there to admit Mr Donaldson as minister of Rathven. Cullen, 22nd September, 4 o'clock p.m.-The Presbytery met, and, after ringing of the bell, they proceeded to the Church of Cullen, agreeable to former appointment, where, after sermon by Mr Milne, from John iii, 1,2, Mr Donaldson was admitted by him as minister of Rathven."

John Farqumarson was the next minister (1822-25), then came James Gardiner (1825-61), James Crighton (1861-66), formerly minister of the Buckie Chapel; James M'Lachlan (1866-74), James Buchanan (1874-79), and the Rev. G. I. Donald.

CHAPTER VIII

Episcopal History

*W*e will now return to the Episcopalians, having parted company with Mr Crammond's valuable extracts from the minutes of the Presbytery of Fordyce. Mr Longmuir's successor was probably the Rev. James Willox. At any rate, in a list of clergy of the Diocese of Aberdeen at this period, which appeared in an Aberdeen newspaper in 1865, that gentleman's name is given in connection with the charge at Rathven. How long Mr Willox's ministry in Rathven lasted we do not know; but amongst the subscribers to "The Ancient Liturgy of the Church of Jerusalem," published in 1744, we find the name of the "Rev. Mr William Mitchell at Arradoul." Before this date , a church had been built near Arradoul, on the bank of the Burn of Buckie, close to the eighteenth milestone on the old road from Banff. This church was burnt down by the Duke of Cumberland's army in 1746, on their way to Culloden. An aged member of the Church at Buckie, now upwards of fourscore-and-ten years of age, tells how her grandfather ventured to approach the smoking ruins in the evening from under cover of the surrounding furze, and, with his staff, rescued portions of the prayer books from the smouldering pile. The smoke he described as rising up to heaven, calling for vengeance.

After the burning of their church, the Episcopalians of Rathven met for divine worship in a kiln on the farm of Barrhill. Here they were one day surprised by the authorities, and the heads of families taken before the Sheriff-Substitute at Banff. Like the two grandchildren of St. Jude, when brought before the Roman Emperor, they showed their horny hands, and their spokesman (he who rescued portions of the prayer books from the burning church) pleaded that they were poor simple country folk, incapable of harming anyone, and that they were not aware of breaking any law when they met for Divine worship. The Sheriff, who at heart was not unfriendly, dismissed them with a caution, at the same time advising them to keep their meetings very quiet, and occasionally to attend the Presbyterian Church, selecting a conspicuous position in it. Thus warned, it was necessary for the Rathven churchmen to exercise more caution. Accordingly, Mr Mitchell used to travel from house to house and repeat divine service in each. On Sunday evenings the young people would steal under cover of the darkness to Mr Mitchell's house at Barrhill - a thatched cottage by the way - to be catechised. A hairy trunk stood in the corner of the reverend gentleman's room, and whoever distinguished himself or herself in repeating the Catechism was rewarded with a quarter of oat cakes taken from the trunk. Mr Mitchell's ministrations extended as far as Portsoy on the east and Fochabers on the west, both of these congregations being dependent upon him for services. A few of the tokens cast during Mr Mitchell's pastorate are still in existence, and also one of those cast during the pastorate of Mr John Hay - he who was deprived of the Rathven Church at the revolution.

The baptismal registers of the Arradoul congregation are preserved among the other papers of the Church of Buckie. They date back as far as 1757. From that date to 1779, two registers were kept, the first containing a list of "Baptisms of riper years," and the second a list of infant baptisms. Between 1757 and 1779 there were no fewer than ninety-one baptisms of riper years. The first five of these took place at one time, "immediately before a confirmation by Bishop Falconer." On another occasion, in 1775, we find Bishop Kilgour acting as one of the witnesses. A number of the earlier of the baptisms show how severe the persecution of the Episcopal Church had been, and also that the penal enactments were now beginning to be less strictly enforced. The rest, being the baptism of converts, show that, in the opinion of the churchmen of these days, Presbyterian baptism was invalid. The late Roman Catholic bishop, Bishop Kyle, who died at Enzie, used to say that he had no hesitation in accepting Episcopalian baptism as valid, because it was so carefully administered; but that he could not accept Presbyterian baptism, on account of the slovenly manner in which it was performed. The register records the baptism in 1771, of Helen, daughter of, - and in 1772 of John, son of the Rev. Andrew Macfarlane, Newmill, afterwards Bishop of Moray. The Roman Catholics, with the connivance of the parish minister, restored St. Margaret's Chapel of the Craigs in 1765, and the Episcopalians of Rathven must have erected a place of worship soon after, for in August 1772, James Bennet was baptised the second day after birth "at the Chapel of Arradoul."

Arradoul is on the estate of Cairnfield, and Mr Alexander Gordon, the laird, must have been a true and devoted churchman before he would have run the risk involved - no small one in those days of penal enactments - in granting a resting-place to the persecuted Church. Further, by a deed of mortification, dated October 21, 1763, he endowed the Episcopal Church in Elgin and the Episcopal Church at Arradoul with "one half quarter and auchteen part of the town and lands," along with houses, etc., of Barflathills, near Elgin. The proportion of rent from this farm paid to Buckie at the present time amounts to £15 per annum.

The chapel at Arradoul must have been of a very temporary and unpretending character. The Roman Catholic chapel in the neighbourhood was erected for the modest sum of thirteen guineas, and the Episcopal chapel is not likely to have cost more. Dr Neale, in his life of Bishop Torry, speaks of it as a kitchen; for he says that when Mr Torry was appointed to the charge at Arradoul in 1782 the congregation assembled for divine service in his kitchen, as being the largest room in the house. Dean Ranken, in his "Sketches of the History of the Church of Scotland from the period of the Reformation," writes:- "Among the last of the clergy whom I have known who had been forced to worship God in the hidden make-shift way I have mentioned, was Dr Patrick Torry, Bishop of St Andrews, Dunkeld, and Dunblane, who died at Peterhead in extreme old age so late as 1852. I have heard the Bishop tell that, when a young priest at Arradoul in the Enzie - now represented by the Buckie congregation - he had been forced to celebrate the Holy Communion on the table of a farm kitchen, hastily scoured, and prepared for the occasion." Matters, however, were not allowed to remain long in this unsatisfactory state, for in the Presbytery minutes of 1783 it is recorded that "the Roman Catholics and non-jurors have lately obtained very genteel accommodation for their congregations." The "genteel accommodation" provided in the new church at Arradoul may readily be imagined when it is stated that, within the memory of persons still alive, the seats consisted principally of forms and planks. The church stood east and west, and there was an entrance at each end, with a passage running along the centre. The pulpit stood against the north wall, and under it was the altar in the middle of the church. In the early part of the present century the church was fitted up with high-backed pews, and with a few of those large square boxes, seated all round. Though the pews were thus well adapted for a quiet sleep, it was not always safe to indulge in one. Mr Murdoch, Keith, happening to officiate one Sunday, is said to have planted a well-aimed blow with his knotted red handkerchief on the head of an unlucky wight who was rude enough to snore during the sermon. Mr Torry continued at Arradoul till 1789, when he removed to Peterhead.

Mr Torry was succeeded at Arradoul by the Rev. Alexander Shand, who afterwards became Dean of the Diocese of Aberdeen. Mr Shand was a native of Forgue. He came to

Arradoul from Peterhead, having exchanged with Mr Torry. It is said that he considered he had rather a grievance against the future Bishop of St Andrews for having induced him to make the exchange. Mr Shand was of small stature, quick temperament, keen at making a bargain when selling the produce of his farm, hateful of all waste, and very kind and charitable to the poor. He was very much prejudiced against surplices, and used stoutly to declare that he would never wear one. But alas! for human consistency; even the Dean had eventually to comply, and wear the hated garment. The first Sunday that he wore it he hung his head, as, ill-at-ease, he rapidly strode along the passage of the church, pulling the surplice tightly round him. Others in the Enzie beside Dean Shand have eventually had to make a right-about face. The late minister of the Established Church had a notable sermon, well known in the surrounding parishes, in which there occurred the passage:- "Awa' wi' your organs an' your orchestras, an' a' that;" but on the Duke of Richmond, after the restoration of the ducal chapel at Fochabers, presenting the organ of that chapel to the kirk, the worthy minister discarded the old sermon for one in praise of organs. Dean Shand was well versed in the Roman controversy, and used regularly once a year to preach on the subject. When any of his flock married a Roman Catholic and joined the Roman Church his man-servant was wont to say- "We ken what the minister will be on next Sunday" And, sure enough, the sermon on the following Sunday was a scathing denunciation of Popery. Dean Shand supplied services at Fochabers, but latterly became so infirm that he could not be trusted to make the journey alone.

Dean Shand was succeeded at Arradoul by the Rev. Edward Lillingston, an English clergyman. Mr Lillingston was an eloquent preacher of the Evangelical school, and very popular. He was noted in the district for the horses which he kept, and for his skill in riding and driving. He used to ride to Elgin, a distance of fifteen miles, in an hour, and return in the same short time. A horse that could not do that, he said, was not worth keeping. He married a daughter of Mr Gordon of Cairnfield, who built a large and commodious house for his use close to the church. After a brief stay in Scotland (from May 20, 1835 to December 4, 1836) Mr Lillingston returned to England where he became a rural dean.

The next incumbent was the Rev. John Moir, now Dean of Glasgow. It was he who first began to hold services in Buckie. A building formerly occupied by the Wesleyans, and which was afterwards bought by Bishop William Skinner for £75 for the use of the congregation, was rented by him, and service held in it on Sunday afternoons. The building contained 200 sittings, and stood in Low Street on the site of the house occupied by Mrs Thomson, vintner. The chapel at Arradoul had 211 sittings. The Wesleyans were at one time very strong in Buckie, but through the tippling propensity of the members, many of whom were struck off the roll for having been intoxicated, the membership gradually decreased until the charge was abandoned, the rules in regard to drink being very strict. John Wesley having declared that the drink traffic was blasted at both ends and cursed in the middle.

Mr Moir was succeeded in 1840 by the Rev. William Christie, who was the last incumbent at Arradoul, and eventually became Dean of Moray. In 1844, through a misunderstanding, the church at Arradoul was shut up, by which the congregation was greatly scattered.

The next incumbent was the Rev. Alexander Troup, and then the Rev. Alexander Temple, now of Armdale. Lastly came the Rev. J. R. Leslie, who was appointed in July, 1884, and in July 1887 accepted a unanimous call to the incumbency of S. James', Muthill, Perthshire. Principally by his efforts the present beautiful church in Buckie, consecrated on 1st November, 1876, was built. In the following year a parsonage was also erected.

CHAPTER IX

Roman Catholic History

From a report to Propaganda in 1677 by Mr Alex. Leslie, we learn that the small number of Catholics in the Lowlands was thus distributed:- Galloway contained 550; Glasgow and its neighbourhood, 50; Forfarshire and Kincardineshire, 72; Aberdeenshire, 405; Banffshire, 1000; and Morayshire, 8.

Mr Leslie, it is said, was sometimes forewarned of approaching danger, during the heat of persecution, by a preternatural shaking of his bed as he lay asleep at night. Once, in particular, when residing in Glastirum House, his bed began to shake. He rose in consequence and struck a light. That night there were several parties of soldiers scouring the Enzie in quest of priests, but, seeing a light at that hour at Glastirum, a noted haunt of the Catholic clergy, and a central object through the Enzie, they imagined that a party of their comrades was already there, and therefore thought it unnecessary to search in that direction.

In 1690 the principal Roman Catholic station in Scotland was in the Enzie. Preshome was the ordinary residence of the Prefect of the Mission, and afterwards, of the Bishop, when he was not actually engaged in his frequent visitations. The Protestants called the Enzie "the Papistical Country. "The meetings of the clergy were often held there, the influence of the Duke of Gordon disposing the Privy Council to leniency as regarded that district. Since the beginning of the 17th century the Parish of Rathven has given no fewer than eight bishops to the R.C. Church., viz:- James Gordon, born at Glastirum; James Grant, born at Wester Bogs; John Geddes, born at Corriedown; Alexander Paterson, born at Pathhead; Andrew Scott, born at Chapelford; John Murdoch, born at Wellheads; Alex. Smith, born at Wester Bogs; and John Gray, who was born in a small house which stood on a site now included within the walls of the present Established Church in Buckie; and in the immediate neighbourhood, Thomas Nicolson, born at Birkenbog; and Alex. Smith, born in the old village of Fochabers.

A Roman Catholic Chapel is mentioned as having been in ruins at St. Ninian's early in the 17th century. In 1687 there were two Catholic clergymen residing in the Enzie - Alexander Leslie, alias "Hardboots," and John Irvine, alias "Cabrach." Both resided at Walkerdale, which the Prefect had purchased. The two clergymen were engaged under the auspices of Alexander, the last Catholic Duke of Gordon, in building a chapel in the centre of the churchyard, dedicated to St. Ninian. Though not quite finished it was made use of by September, 1688; and continued in use for 37 years. In a letter by Alexander Winster, Prefect, and signed by him and eight others while met in council at Gordon Castle, April 16, 1688, he mentions that "in the midst of the countrie there is a large chapel built, or rather building, capable to contain 1000 persons, on the old found of St. Ninian's Chapel."

In September, 1725, one Morison, aided by a share of the £1000 said to have been given by King George to the General Assembly to aid in evangelising the most Catholic districts, came to Gordon Castle on a Saturday of that month. On the same day arrived James Carnegy, the priest. Morison, it seems, requested the use of St. Ninian's Chapel for the purpose of conducting worship on the following day according to the Protestant belief. The request was refused by the Duke on the ground that it had been built chiefly at his cost, and was a burial place of his family and servants. Next day, however, Morison collected a body of hearers, and broke open a window, and put in a boy who unfastened the door. At the close of this service he stated his intention to repeat the same on the following Sunday. On Monday the Earl of Findlater, sheriff of the shire, dined at Gordon Castle, when he was asked and promised to prevent this proceeding. The Catholics, however, did not place much faith in the Earl's promise, and the Duke sent a notary with two gentlemen on the following Sunday to take evidence. The intruders finding door and windows repaired and barricaded conducted worship outside; while a party, said to have come from Fochabers and neighbourhood - tradition adds, with blackened faces, so as to prevent identification - gathered round them, and, against the orders of the Duke's servants, assailed and wounded some, and drove the whole from the field. This incident created a good deal of commotion, and serious consequences were threatened, but Alexander, Duke of Gordon, went to London to propitiate the Government; and nothing more was heard of the matter. The Catholics, however, never ventured to make further use of it. It fell again into ruin; and long afterwards the slates were employed in roofing the chapel at Tynet. Every trace of the old chapel, except the foundation, has now disappeared; but the churchyard is being carefully preserved. Independent of the beauty of the natural scenery, the spot possesses great interest to a Scottish Catholic; for here are the remains of Bishop Nicolson, the first Vicar Apostolic in Scotland; as also the remains of 24 missionary priests, of whose burials there are records. The Rev. Archibald Anderson, a deacon, son of the last laird of Tynet, is also interred in St. Ninian's. The bishop and clergy are buried on the site of the chancel in the old chapel. While workmen were engaged about four years ago taking down the pillars of the previous entrance to St. Ninian's Churchyard, they came upon the keystone of the old chapel door, which bears the date 1687. From the shape of the stone it is evident that the doorway was a rounded arch. This interesting remnant of the past was built into the wall of the churchyard, to the left of the gateway, and in a position to be easily seen by anyone within the ground. It is in an excellent state of preservation.

The Duke above referred to died, it is said, from the effects of his hurried journey to London in connection with the Sunday disturbance at St. Ninian's. The body of the Duke lay in state in the Chapel of St. Ninian's surrounded by numerous candles; which was the last use to which the chapel was put. Two large pillars of wood, painted as marble, which had stood at each corner of the altar, were latterly removed to Tynet, and finally discarded by the late Rev. Mr Loggie, being reduced to a mere painted shell with the dry rot. The Duke kept a priest at Gordon Castle, and the Duchess a Protestant clergyman; and occasionally disputes arose at table between them, in which the Protestant generally won his case by keeping his temper.

Another chapel, called the Chapel of the Craigs, seemed shortly afterwards to have been built. It stood a little way above Cairnfield, and about half a mile to the eastward of the priest's residence at Preshome. It was gutted by the English soldiers on their return march from Culloden in 1747, and the books and vestments carried to Cullen, and burnt in the Market Place.

After the destruction of the Chapel of the Craigs, the congregation assembled in great privacy in a small room at Preshome.

About the year 1760, Mr George Hay, afterwards Bishop Hay, took steps for restoring the old Chapel of the Craigs. He made several visits to Rannas, the seat of his distant relation, to sound that family on the subject, and secure their influence with Mr Grant, the parish minister, so that no obstacle might be put in the way. His friends at

Rannas, though Protestants, entered cheerfully into the plan, and obtained an assurance from Mr Grant that he would assist Mr Hay by every means in his power and even give timely warning if the Presbytery took up the matter and decided to take hostile steps. Mr Grant thereupon removed all his property from the chapel; and a few men were hired to put it in repair and roof it in. If an outcry had been raised in the neighbourhood, it was agreed to desist from doing anything further. Little public attention was paid to the matter; and by the end of December, 1765, the congregation were again worshipping in the Chapel of the Craigs. It contained a gallery twelve feet long. The entire expense was only a little over thirteen guineas. After it was reopened for service, Mr Hay was one Sunday about to begin mass, when some one who had, as usual, been set to keep watch outside, reported that a soldier was seen approaching. Mr Hay immediately withdrew into the wood adjoining till he was informed that the alarm was a false one; the bright scarlet waistcoat of a citizen of Fochabers having been mistaken for a soldier's uniform.

On May 23, 1791, a new chapel (founded in 1788) was opened at Preshome, principally through the liberality of Mr Alex. Gordon of Letterfourie. No chapel approaching to it in pretensions had been erected in Britain since the Reformation. A tablet over the principal entrance, towards the west, announces its dedication in 1788, the year in which the foundation was laid. The chapel is a large, plain building, erected by Rev. John Reid, and has been several times repaired and altered outside and inside, besides having a gallery removed.

Newlands, Auchinhalrig, or Tynet Chapel, by the way, is perhaps the oldest in Scotland, and still retains its pristine simplicity. It is even more interesting than Preshome from its associations. It was built in 1771 by Rev. Dr Alex. Geddes, professedly as a sheep cot, and to avoid suspicion sheep were now and then put into it, and these made a superior puddled floor. Finally it was roofed in, and used as a chapel. Six years afterwards, in 1777, Dr Geddes was engaged building a chapel at Fochabers at which time the Duke of Gordon was transferring the villages from the immediate neighbourhood of Gordon Castle to the present site. Dr Geddes's chapel took the place of the one that existed in the old village. It was built at the north-east corner of Fochabers and was succeeded by the present building, erected in 1828 by Mr George Mathieson, who died a few months before it was opened by Bishop Paterson.

In 1831 or 1832, owing to the increase in the numbers of Roman Catholics in the district, and the long distance many of them had to walk to Preshome, it was thought advisable to hold service in Buckie. Accordingly, the Society's hall in Cluny Square (now occupied by Messrs Duncan and Graham) was rented for two years and afterward purchased. It was continued to be used until the opening of the present church in 5th July, 1857. The building was an exceedingly costly one, and is very handsome. The Rev. W. Clapperton was appointed to the charge, and a year or two ago was promoted to the rural deanship.

CHAPTER X

The Burn of Buckie

*T*he postal address of the people living near the mouth of the Burn of Buckie a century ago was the Shore of Buckie. In fact, this designation was understood to embrace all the houses built within the present area of the town. The name Buckie, by the way, unlike most of the names of the other places in the district, which are of Gaelic derivation, is obviously of German origin, being derived from Bucht, a bay. The name of the parish, Rathven, is said to be derived from the Gaelic word brake or fern, and from rock, eminence, or hillock. During this century the immediate line of coast has undergone some very remarkable changes. These were brought about by natural causes and the industry of man. The Burn of Buckie, before the period of harbours in this quarter, was an estuary of considerable depth. Boats and small coasting vessels could sail up the Burn some hundred yards - nearly as far as the present railway bridge - and find a good shelter in rough weather. It is narrated that during a storm about the year 1828 three vessels made together for the Burn mouth, without having a pilot on board. Two of them arrived in safety, but the third being too far to the west, became a total wreck. Of course, a stone bridge across the Burn was not then in existence. Instead, two or three planks, with a crazy rail on one side, did duty for a roadway. This apology for a bridge was on the site of the present structure, and of course could only be used by pedestrians. It was raised to such a height that it allowed boats to pass under it with lowered masts, or for that matter its removal was the work of only a few minutes. Carts and other vehicles could only get across the Burn when the tide was out. The shallowest place was at the mouth of the Burn, and here the carts crossed, passing round the end of the "Stane House" when going east, and proceeding along the road in the Yardie close to the beach.

The Yardie

The pedestrians who crossed by the "bridge" proceeded by a foot road along the foot of the brae. There were then (about 1823) only three houses in the Yardie - the Old Stane Hoos, Mr Kessock's, and Mr Wiseman's. The Stane House is an ancient building - in fact, was one of the principal buildings, and is accredited with being the first slated house in the town. Not a few vessels have discharged cargoes alongside it. When it was built, or for what purpose, no one now, we believe, can tell. It has been utilised for a great many purposes. About 120 years ago it was occupied by a merchant who was known as "Provost" Lamb. The "Provost" was a gentleman a little over three feet in height, and it is said that on one occasion when serving a customer with treacle he fell headlong into the cask, and thereby almost came to an untimely end. He latterly removed to the house occupied by Mr Williamson, china merchant. At another period the Stane House was used as a tobacco manufactory, and then it came into the hands of an English company who purchased cod roe to send to England. On the night when Prince Charlie was born it is said that the north-west corner of it was washed down by a gale. A good many years ago it was heightened by Mr Jamieson, fishcurer, and had a stone staircase on the south side which led to the upper lat. On the west side of the Burn there was a building known by the name of the Little Stane House, which was used as a cooperage by Mr Alex. Thomson, and was of even older date.

Buckie Burn Bridges

Reference has been made to the bridge which spanned the Buckie Burn near its mouth. Humble as it was, it was much better than none. The wooden planks latterly gave place to a stone bridge, which was erected by public subscription, but was demolished by the spate of 1829. A second - the present - stone bridge was then built. The bridge leading from West Church Street to Nether Buckie is of a later date. Uncomfortable as the idea must have been of crossing the planks at the mouth of the Buckie Burn in a dark and stormy night, it was undoubtedly more dangerous to cross the Burn at a point little below the West Church Street bridge. Narrow footpaths on each side ran down to the water's edge, and the Burn was crossed by the pedestrian on a few stepping stones, perhaps covered with sods. A false step, and a ducking was the inevitable reward. When it is remembered, too, that burns were haunted by fairies - or were said to be - the horror of crossing at this point at night must have been a strain almost altogether too great for the mind of the superstitious to endure. It was not a time for too precipitate movements, either in crossing on the stones or descending or ascending the paths. Of course, every time the Burn was swollen by rain the stones were washed away, and a new crossing had to be made.

But to return to the Yardie. In 1823 every available part of it was arable land. From Mr Kessock's house to the Burn a fine crop of barley was yearly to be seen. The name Yardie, it is said, is derived from the fact that fishermen had small plots of ground on the east side. It is further stated that a little over a hundred years ago a small thatched house on the south end of Mr Kessock's house was used as a sheep cot by the farmer - or the laird - of Rannas. Mr Kessock's house in its earliest days was a public house, and was the scene of not a few festive gatherings - marriage parties, etc. - and a recess is shown in the wall of a large room where the fiddlers sat and played their merriest jigs while the company danced with right good will.

Harbours

What the fishermen at the beginning of this century used to call the harbour was a pier built partly of wood and partly of stone, which ran out at a point between the present east pier and the Burn. This pier could be utilised on either side. Every vestige of the erection has long ago disappeared. There was another wooden pier with a stone point which went out from below Philip's Inn. It was only about four feet in breadth. Until very recently some of the woodwork of this pier could be seen above the beach, some feet in height. There is a great alteration in the appearance of the houses in this quarter since the beginning of the century. Most of the old houses had a door in the gable, and the spray has been seen coming down the chimneys of several of them. A few of the houses, indeed, were washed away by the sea, and a stone bulwark had to be placed at the back of the Gordon Arms to prevent it sharing a similar fate. Harbour accommodation coming to be much required, through the agency of the late Rev. Mr Shanks, a wooden harbour was erected at the Hythie in 1843. The reverend gentleman very often "gaffered" the men himself, and it was no unusual sight for him to be seen with a pick or shovel in his hand. Each boat's crew contributed so much towards the undertaking, but the pier was rather low and possessed little or no weight to counterbalance the buoyancy of the timber, so that in the course of half-a-dozen years a storm washed it away. This was a severe blow to Mr Shanks, who had to pay the most of the money out of his own pocket for its erection. It possessed a good depth of water, and was considered a fine harbour so long as it stood. It received no repairs after its erection, a fact which doubtless hastened its demolition.

Thus much, then, for wooden harbours. They were of the greatest utility to the fishermen, but were not built in such a manner as to be a shelter to the boats from the violence of the storm. When a storm was seen brewing the boats had to be hauled up on the beach, as the result was, that if caught lying at moorings, they were tossed on the shore and wrecked. Consequently, when overtaken in a storm it was useless to think of making the harbour. The boats sought the shelter of the Craigenroan, or ran ashore at the Salters (the site of the Cluny Harbour) where they were sheltered to a small extent by the Mucks, and a ledge of rocks that ran in the same direction as the north pier of the harbour. Many crews, however, have perished because they had no properly sheltered nook to fly to when they neared the shore. Their last refuge was the Cromarty Firth, and once inside the Soutars they were safe; but there is a long stretch before Cromarty is reached, and numbers perished before they could attain that place of safety.

The limited harbour accommodation caused not a few fishermen to seek "pastures new," and many went to other ports. But the Nether Buckie Harbour, begun in 1855, stayed the exodus, and in fact was the chief cause of the development of the fishing industry in the district, and raised Buckie to a first place as a fishing town. A stone in the pier of the Nether Buckie Harbour bears the following inscription:- "Erected by the Board of Fisheries, Edinburgh, and Robert Gordon, Esq., Letterfourie. Begun 1855; finished 1857. Engineers, D. & T. Stevenson. Resident engineer, William Middlemas. Contractor, Alexander Stuart." Whatever may be the most objectionable feature of the harbour, as regards stability it has been a monument of engineering science. For about 30 years it has withstood the force of many wild storms, and has never received the least repair. When the ordnance survey was being taken in this district the engineers were highly pleased with the manner the harbour was built. Having to make some marks on the sea wall in connection with their levels, "Why," remarked one, "the stones of this harbour are as hard as flint." The stones, it may be remarked, were brought from the Hopeman district. The inside face of the sea walls and the packing are of hard primary rock from the shore between Portessie and Findochty, and the original Roman cement pointing still holds tenaciously to the joints on the sea wall. The Burn has proved a very bad neighbour to the harbour by sending large quantities of gravel across the mouth and thereby greatly lessening the depth of water. An attempt is at present being made to obtain the loan of money, with the object of having the harbour deepened and enlarged. It is to be hoped that the negotiations will end satisfactorily, and the works be successfully carried out.

1880 saw the fine Cluny Harbour completed at a cost of £65,000. It occupied from five to six years in erection, and for depth of water is scarcely to be surpassed by any harbour on the east coast of Scotland, including Aberdeen, Dundee, and Leith. The total harbour area at command, however, is still inadequate to the needs of the fishermen of the district.

CHAPTER XI

The Regality of Huntly
We are indebted to the research of Mr Crammond, Cullen,
for the following:-

*O*ne of the original Court Books of the Regality of Huntly, of date 1721-1733, is preserved in the General Register House, Edinburgh, and serves to give some idea of the administration of justice in the district of Buckie when Buckie itself was but in its infancy [it was written with a small "b" in those days]. The Duke of Gordon was Lord of Regality, and in the earlier part of the period referred to George Cumin, younger of Recletich, was baillie. In 1731 Cosmo George, Duke of Gordon, appointed George Gordon of Buckie, baillie; and John Gordon of Auchinreath was baillie-depute. There were several other Courts within the Regality, those being presided over by other baillies. For example, Courts were regularly held at Huntly, and a Court Book for that district from 1679 to 1711 is also preserved in the Register House, besides Court records for Badenoch and Lochaber. The districts that lay within the jurisdiction of George Cumin and George Gordon were the lands and lordship of Enzie, the barony of Fochabers, Coldhame, and Ordiwhich. The Courts were held usually at Fochabers or Gordon Castle, but the baillie had power to hold them at any place within his jurisdiction. The prison was at Boghead. Heritable jurisdictions were abolished in Scotland about fourteen years after the period when this book closes. The following extracts will furnish some general idea of the character of the cases that came before the Court. Not a few of them from Buckie and elsewhere were cases of debt, bills, etc. One of the first cases is an action by Mr M'Culloch, minister of the parish of Bellie, against a parishioner for non-payment of the usual fine imposed by the kirk sessions in a certain class of cases that came frequently before them. The accused pleaded that the case occurred before 24th July, 1721, and that he was therefore freed by His Majesty's most gracious pardon. The baillie assoilzied him. Soon after, Mr M'Culloch had no less than nine cases of a similar character before the Court. Three escaped on the same ground as the last; but, in the case of the others, decree was granted for the penalties imposed by the Kirk Session, which varied from £5 to £20 Sc. each.

1722, July 19. Decree given in an action - Alexander, Duke of Gordon, against Alexander Derge, Carter in Shoar of Buckie, for sex hunder dozen of haddocks, being custom fish payable out of His Grace's six boats of Buckie and received by the defender for three years and a month; as also for eight hunder and sixteen dozen of custom haddocks due out of Buckie boats for the said time, having got allowance of a month's fish of everie boat yearly for ill weather. The said haddock at 2 shillings Scots per dozen. The defender present and confessing.

1722, Aug. 13. Alexander Dason in Carnefeild, James Milne in Oran, and Andrew Machattie in Pethhead amerciat in £10 Scots for winning of fir in the Red Moss.

1722, Nov. 23. Decreet Alexander Anderson of Arradoul against John Wilson in Littleburn of Buckie for £7 10s for six firlots meall at £5 Sc. per boll.

1723, March 13. Andrew Jamieson at Shoar of Buckie renounced his possession of houses, yard, and land in Nether Buckie to and in favours of the Duke of Gordon.

1723, July 30. Alexander Forbes at Shoar of Buckie for beating in the head with a grape James Simpson, son to John Simpson in Tarbuckie, is amerciat £20 Scots.

Andrew Forsyth is decerned to pay £1 10s as price of a firlot bear to William Geddes in Nether Buckie.

1723, Dec 11. The Bailzie amerciates Robert Innes in £100 Sc. for killing of a rae, by dogs, in time of storm, and in £10 for cutting of green wood, with £20 of damages.

1724. John Gordon in Fochabers, is amerciat in £10 Sc. for beating and blooding James Miln ther.

John Straton, mason in Fochabers, is amerciat in £2 Scots for contumacy in not appearing as a witness when cited.

Thomas Miln, Fochabers, is amerciat in £50 Sc. for beating John Gordon, shoemaker in Fochabers, with ane cart bar.

John Brander, at Sawmiln of Fochabers, is ordained to pay four merks as the price of four lambs and £1.10s as the price of a ewe killed by his dog.

1724. Action by the park-keeper to the Duke of Gordon against Isobel Shand in Fochabers for three shillings four pennies for each head of 30 of sheep found in the parks of Gordon Castle, for which the said keeper drew a plaid as poind. Besides the above payment she is amerciat in 12s Scots for her servant Margaret Halden leaping the park dyke.

Decreet given in an action, Andrew Geddes in Burnside, against James Angus at Shoar of Buckie, for £9 as the price of six firlots malt.

1724, July 30. Decreet given in an action, Alexander Ranken, Merchant, Fochabers, against Alexander Tod, in Upper Auchinreath, for four shillings starlin as the price of a book borrowed by the defender from the pursuer, the book being ane octavo, and treating upon the controversy 'twixt the Papists and Protestants. Defender is present and confesses his borrowing the book, but that Mr Thomas M'Culloch, minister of Bellie, took the book out of his house when he was from home.

1724, Aug. 8. Decreet given in an action, Walter S., wigmaker and barber at Fochabers, against Bessie Barclay there, for two pound Sc. yearly for five years, for shaving of the said Bessie Barclay her head.

John Innes, late servant to a shoemaker in Fochabers, is fined £20 Scots for breaking the garden dykes of Gordon Castle and stealing fruit. Also £24 Sc. as the price of said fruits and for damage to the dykes and trees, and that he be caryed to the prison at Boghead, there to lie at his own charges and expenses till payment be made or security given. "He went in over the garden gate at Whytefield about 11 acloak at night, and did pull and carry away some of the best whyte globbs or goosberrys and a considerable quantity of fyn apprecoits and peaches of the vall'd trees and the finest pears and aples he could find in the garden both from the wall and standart trees.

1724. John Robertson, Merchant in Nether Buckie, obtains decree against John Robertson, merchant in Fochabers, for £6 19s 6d.

1725, Feb. 6. Peter Slater, servant to Peter Taylor in Netherbucky, and Janet Green, servant to said Peter Taylor, are amerciat in £4 Sc., ilk ane of them for beating and blooding of one another.

1725, Ap. 5. Gilbert Knight, Fochabers, is fined £40 Sc. for carrying fire near to a fir park lately planted containing 500,000 fir trees belonging to the Duke of Gordon.

1727, Jan. 11. Decreet Katherine Burnet, Lady Bucky, and her husband for his intrest against James Jack, weaver in Upper Auchinreath, decerning him to weave to her against the 1st May nixt to cum, the number of 21 ells of Dornich nepery under the falzie of 20s Scots each ell, and five ells and ane half of dornich table cloths under the falzie of 48s per ell. The defender present and craving that the samen had been warped 20 months ago.

CHAPTER XII

Smuggling

The expensive wars of the eighteenth and beginning of nineteenth century caused an extraordinary drain on the national purse, and the Government was compelled to levy money on almost every article of commerce, from the luxuries of civilisation down to the bare necessaries to sustain life. Such a state of things could not have been otherwise than productive of much evil and suffering. It is not to be wondered at, then, that smuggling should have flourished as an industry - that men should have endeavoured to evade paying the heavy Government duties, and made smuggling an established trade. Men of good moral character felt no qualms of conscience in engaging in their illegal occupation. Even the landed gentry thought it no dishonour to be connected with a business which, though dangerous, was often highly remunerative. The whole coastside population benefited by smuggling more or less, getting goods free of duty at anyrate, and consequently the excise officers had a united public to bargain with in the execution of their duty. Many a smart seaman was engaged on smuggling vessels, for it often required the greatest presence of mind to hoodwink revenue cutters at sea and gaugers on shore. One of the most noted smugglers on the Moray Firth was a celebrated laird whose estate was in the vicinity of Burghead. He carried on smuggling with much success, hiding his contraband goods in the caves which abound at that part of the coast. Many traditions still live among the people of the Burghead district as to the laird's wonderful adventures and splendid achievements. In Portsoy the chief smuggler was a man named Simpson. Latterly he had been very unsuccessful. With the view of retrieving his fortune he made what he intended as his last smuggling trip, and was on his way home with a full cargo when he was overtaken by a storm and never more heard of. The date on which he was supposed to be lost was the 19th of January, 1834, the day on which two fathers and three sons belonging to Sandend were drowned. Along the coast, from Portsoy to Cullen, great quantities of smuggled goods were landed, some of the creeks near the old Castle of Findlater being specially suited for the purpose, the caves providing capital concealment. There is a tradition that the Fish-house Cave at Findlater penetrates as far as the Binn Hill. At Sandend the capacious public-house kept by Mrs Hacket, situated quite close to the creek where the boats land their fish, was a well-known place of concealment. All along the coast, everything on which duty was levied was smuggled. Holland Gin, however, was the principal trade. The casks contained from eight to nine gallons. Also, there were numerous stills up the country, and whisky, etc., was brought down to the coastside and sold. In Nether Buckie for a few years the manufacture of snuff was engaged in unknown to the excise officers.

A great deal of smuggling went on in salt along the coast. Not over 50 years ago salt cost as high as 4s per bushel; and £3 per ton, wholesale price, not including duty. What is purchased now for 2d would then have cost 10d. Fishcurers and the skippers of boats had each a salt bond cellar. The door was provided with a couple of locks, one of the keys of which was kept by the gauger, and the other was the property of the owner of the salt. By this system it was intended that salt should not be taken out of the cellar save in the presence of the Customs officials. Therefore, when salt was required by a fishcurer, or by a skipper for himself and crew, notice had to be given to the excisemen or, in their absence, to the tidewaiter. The keys were inserted by the respective parties in the locks, the salt was handed out, and a note taken of the quantity for the purpose of levying the duty. But, notwithstanding all precautions, great quantities were smuggled. The excisemen were particular in watching women bound for the country, or Elgin or Keith, professedly to sell fish; but on their creels being inspected it was found as often as not that the major part of their burden was composed of salt. In such a case, the officer would take the creel and scatter the salt on the road or confiscate it. It was no unusual sight to see every quarter of a mile between Buckie and Portgordon, on the high road to Elgin, a quantity of salt scattered across the road. The abuse the zealous officers received now and then from these sturdy fisherwomen can be more easily imagined than described.

The principal in nearly the whole of the smuggling transactions that took place in the neighbourhood of Buckie was George Geddes, or Captain Geddes as he was popularly known, from the fact that he was captain of a company of volunteers, or militia as they were called, whose usual drill ground was at the back of the Gordon Arms. The Captain was born in Buckie in 1765, and in early life he and his brother Alexander carried on business as shipowners, being the owners of a few coasting vessels. In 1793 the merchants of Buckie were proprietors of four sloops of 18, 25, 30, and 36 tons, and two of 60 tons each, the whole navigated by 24 seamen. This was a very fair shipping list for the period in question. The brothers must have felt time hang heavily on their hands but for the fact that they supplemented their business as shipowners by carrying on a very extensive trade in smuggling. Every now and then a vessel brought them a cargo of smuggled goods. The vessels approached the coast during the night, and by a well-arranged system of signalling by lights the crews were informed whether the gaugers were on the look-out, or whether it was expedient to proceed to sea again and wait a more favourable opportunity for landing the cargo. If everything was thought to be safe, boats put off from the shore and the work of unloading was proceeded with very quietly and with great expedition. By daylight the vessel was generally out of sight of land, and no evidence was left to show the work which had been engaged in during the darkness. On boats approaching the vessel they had to give the countersign. To the hail of "Who goes there?" those in the boat replied, "A friend." "Show it then" was asked, and the challenged parties would very probably reply - "Devil, devil, devil." This was not a very elegant pass word. Few had the hardihood in those days to speak of His Satanic Majesty as the "devil," and it therefore better suited the daring spirits actively engaged in smuggling. A list of the more polite titles given to the "Auld Man" is to be found in Burns' "Address to the De'il." On the boats arriving at the beach from the vessel the smuggled goods were put into carts, which proceeded in various directions. Numerous farmers in the district were engaged by the brothers to provide carts for the conveyance of goods. Large quantities were taken to the moss of Letterfourie, Greenmoss, Redmoss, etc., and hid. Every conceivable place was utilised for hiding the smuggled goods, such as the fishermen's yards, stacks of corn, growing corn, etc. A great many of the houses were built with secret receptacles for the secretion of the smuggled liquor. In a house in Findochty a baking "girdle" was placed against the wall, and few preventive men, it may be calculated, would have thought that it covered the entrance to an aperture, but such was the case. We have mentioned a small building in the Yardie which was originally used as a sheep cot. It has an underground cellar, where many a keg of gin is said to have been secreted. It is narrated that a lady almost fell through the floor of a byre in Nether Buckie, whereby a large underground apartment was discovered, which had undoubtedly been used by the Captain for the requirements of his illicit employment. The Captain had a tobacco manufactory in a house situated on the site of the fishcuring premises of Messrs Gerry in Nether Buckie, and several men were employed by him to make the leaf into roll tobacco. This business he carried on for several years before it was discovered by the excisemen and stopped. One or two raids were made on the house by the officers but until the last occasion he got warning in time to remove every vestige of the unlicensed employment, some of the officers doubtless obtaining a good salary from him to give notice of any proposed raids. Another hiding place may be mentioned, and it is an aperture dug out of the earth in the vicinity of the burn of Rathven, at the point below the churchyard where the footbridge crosses the burn. We believe this receptacle has not been opened or many years. It is carefully covered over with turf, and the only evidence of its existence is to be gleaned from the hollow sound the turf gives back when sharply struck.

In not a few cases quantities of smuggled liquor have been hid so well that they have never been recovered . In the beach near the Burn of Gollachy a whole cargo was said to be hid one night, and somehow or another has never been discovered. It is narrated of a deceased Findochty publican that he often searched in his yard for some liquor that had been hid, and always without success. Doubtless it had been carried off on some occasion by one or more wily individuals who had got scent of the concealed treasure. The incident of a herd lad finding a cask among the sand on the top of the braes between Portgordon and Buckie tells its own tale. The lad tapped the cask and went home "roarin' fou." He hid his find for further use, but missed it next day.

Many amusing stories might be told of the searches undertaken by the officers and the cute expedients taken to throw them off the scent. The excisemen were one day searching at the Bridge End, near where there happened to be a large quantity of unconcealed smuggled stuff, and which it was expected the King's men would light upon. To give time to more securely conceal the goods a ruse was hit upon. The excisemen while proceeding with their search saw a stout woman emerge from a door close by and run up the street carrying a creel from which the end of a barrel protruded. The zealous officers gave chase, which made the woman run faster. When overtaken she screamed out, and asked what they were chasing her for seeing that she was only carrying an empty cask with which to get water for a boat to take to sea. The cask she carried was empty, and during the time the men were away on the wild goose chase after her the goods that were expected to be discovered had been safely concealed.

About the beginning of this century the principal inn in the town was kept by a woman named Mrs Ogilvie, who resided in Nether Buckie. On the occasion of an unexpected visit of the exciseman an anker of smuggled gin was found in her possession, and was accordingly confiscated to the Crown. The proceedings had been observed by a number of workmen, and they set out after the cart which was conveying the gin to Fochabers under the charge of an exciseman who was pretty much the worse of liquor. At the moor of Baremuir, which was then a rather wild-looking place, they quietly took the anker of gin off the cart on which the exciseman was seated, and then disappeared with their prize. The officer soon discovered his loss, and returned to Buckie in a great rage and accused Mrs Ogilvie of having been the instigator of the deed. She denied all knowledge of the transaction, but having an idea who had played the trick she thought it best for her own interests to have the gin restored, which was eventually done.

On another occasion the excisemen had reason to suppose that Mrs Ogilvie had a quantity of smuggled tobacco in her house, and accordingly paid her a visit. The tobacco was generally made up in large round rolls of the shape of a grindstone, and on the occasion of the visit of the excisemen a roll was concealed in the bed under the blankets. The officers intimating that they were to search the bed, Mrs Ogilvie said:- "You can search away, but wait until I take off some of the dirty clothes." Mrs Ogilvie thereupon extended her arms and lifted up the blankets and a roll of tobacco and proceeded to another room. It is needless to say that the men did not discover any tobacco on the premises.

About seventy years ago as a Portessie woman was proceeding along the top of the brae at Nether Buckie, she was stopped by the captain of the preventive men, who asked what she had in her creel. Instead of answering the woman took off her creel and threw it down the brae, when a cask tumbled out. She then rapidly took to her heels, followed by the exciseman. In a short time he returned, having been unable to capture the woman. He expected at least to secure the cask of smuggled liquor; but to his chagrin it had disappeared, having been put into a large pot in which bark was boiling as soon as he got out of sight. The enraged officer's eyes lighted upon a few boys who were standing near watching him with smiling faces indicating that they had seen the whole transaction. The boys were threatened with dire punishment if they did not reveal where the cask had been put, but they proved themselves worthy of the times in which they lived, and refused to answer. In high dudgeon the officer strode off for his men to assist him to search for the cask, but in the meantime the woman returned, the cask was restored to her, and she proceeded home by the top of the town.

In the lentern time the fishing boats more often ventured to the Skate Hole for the purpose of obtaining excisable goods from foreign vessels than for the purpose of fishing. A few of the boats having been caught with smuggled goods on board were forfeited to the Crown and sold or broken up. A boat once arrived at the Hythie with a quantity of stuff, when intimation was made that the King's men were coming. The crew pushed off, and hoisted sail as fast as they could. The officers appearing, fired at the boat and ordered the crew to return. The skipper bawled out to the men to cease firing and that they would do so, the boat all the while pursuing her course for the offing. The boat being undecked the crew managed to hoist the sail, etc., without showing themselves as a target for the excisemen. They easily succeeded in getting clear, and proceeded up the Firth where they found a ready market for their cargo.

On one occasion a Buckie boat arrived at the east side of Findochty with a good consignment of smuggled stuff on board. The crew left the boat and cargo in the charge of a man named John Gaddie, and proceeded to the public house to get "a bottle of ale." Gaddie, instead of watching the boat, proceeded to Portknockie, where a preventive crew were stationed, and informed them of the arrival of the boat. When the Buckie fishermen got back to their craft they found her in the hands of the preventive men. Marching on board the boat the fishermen pitched the preventive men into the water and then set sail for sea. The sequel of the affair was that a party was sent to Buckie to apprehend the crew. The skipper's house was quietly surrounded, but breaking away from those who endeavoured to apprehend him, the skipper rushed out at the door, upsetting two of his would-be captors who confronted him. He managed to escape, and kept out of reach until the matter quietened down. Cases of smuggling were generally tried in Edinburgh. An aged informant mentioned that Cosmo Gordon, a laird of Buckie, was one of "the heads" of the court, and generally paid the fines of the delinquents from Buckie, the sums being light.

It is to be expected that the smuggling vessels now and then would get a pretty sharp chase from the revenue cutters. On one occasion a vessel with a cargo for Captain Geddes was chased by the well-known cutter brig, Prince of Wales. Alexander Slater was the skipper of the smuggling vessel, and kept sail upon her until it often seemed as if she would never rise owing to the quantity of water she shipped. Reaching Noss Head, when out of sight of the brig, Slater ran his vessel into a cave. The cutter coming up thought that the smuggler had gone into Sinclair's Bay, but finding that she was not there it was conjectured that she had foundered from weight of canvas, as the only solution of her sudden disappearance. When darkness came down, Slater came out of the cave and finally managed to reach Buckie and deliver his cargo. Of nine brother of the name of Slater, residing at

Portsoy, it may be remarked, eight of them died while engaged in the smuggling trade. Fishing boats were also now and then chased by Revenue cutters, and not without good reason. On one occasion a Sandend crew, to prevent capture when pursued by a cutter, ran their craft ashore near the mouth of the Spey and took to their heels.

After having been engaged in the smuggling in Buckie for a good many years, Captain Geddes and his brother removed to London, where they successfully carried on the business of shipowners for several years. During the wars the firm chartered ten vessels to the Government for the conveyance of troops. Eight of the vessels were captured, and being uninsured this and other matters helped to ruin them. In one year alone they lost £40,000. It is said, but we do not know if it is correct, that to escape being imprisoned by his creditors, Captain Geddes was conveyed down the Thames in a coffin by a Scotch trading smack. Arrived in Buckie he resumed his old occupation of smuggling, but a coastguard station had meanwhile been established in the town, and at last smuggling as an employment, as at other places, soon came to be a far from remunerative one, and had to be abandoned. The Captain died possessed of little worldly goods, and latterly refused to taste intoxicating liquors. He was a remarkable man, possessed of extensive knowledge, united to a shrewd, persevering, and daring character that fitted him well for the position he occupied - that of the chief of the Buckie smugglers. He left a good many letters, which showed that he had tobacco and rum conveyed from New Orleans to Rotterdam and reshipped for Buckie.

CHAPTER XIII

The Old Houses

A reason has already been given for the higgledy-piggledy order in which the houses in Buckie were built. Another was because the houses being all thatched with straw, shelter was of much importance to prevent the thatching being carried away during a storm. When a gale arose oars and spars were laid on the roof and tied down with ropes. The inside of the houses would have been a curious sight to modern eyes. The light entered through small windows or holes which had a wooden shutter instead of glass, and in cold weather the shutters were closed and light could only enter by a small opening in the roof. No later than 120 years ago, we believe, there was not a pane of glass nor a chimney in the whole of Buckie. The door was low and generally had a step down, the floor, of earth, being lower than the outside ground. The door was fastened in a very primitive fashion. The fastener, or "sneck," was a small piece of hard wood attached with a string to the inside. The "sneck" passed through a staple in the door-post, and thus secured the door. There was generally a small hole like a key-hole near the fastener; and sometimes light-handed persons would get hold of the piece of string that was attached to the "sneck," and noiselessly withdrawing it obtain access to the house. Hence the saying, "a auld sneck-drawer," which was applied to a crafty or stealthy person. Burns called his Satanic Majesty "auld sneck-drawin' doug." The building was generally divided by a partition. The largest part of the house was the kitchen or living part; the "but en' " was commonly called "the cham'er," where the fishing gear, oil, and tar were stored. The furniture was rude and innocent of paint, but clean by much sand-scouring. The principal articles of furniture were the dresser and dishes' rack, which held a great number of soup plates, decorated with blue Chinese pictures. Below were ranged delf bowls of all sizes on which were painted designs of leaves and flowers of brightest colours. Wooden and tin cups, and wooden and horn spoons were also not awanting while under the dresser was the large "pig" that held the treacle, sugar being then very dear. Across the breadth of the kitchen, at the gable, fish were hung on spits to dry and smoke. This was the origin of the fish-kilns. These home-cured fish were famed for their superior quality, and were not excelled. In the houses where the fish were not smoked, the smoke had the freedom of the whole house and family, making its escape through a small aperture in the roof, or by the door. The child's crib was originally a scull for holding lines. Cradles of huge dimensions, however, by and bye came into use, as the following story, told us by an old man, illustrates:- "The press gang always came during the night, with the intention of catching us in our beds. I remember a cutter landing a press gang at Buckie, and the men forthwith proceeded to search the houses. The alarm soon spread, and some of us ran to the hills - some one way and some another. There was one woman folded up her son's legs in a cradle, and put a "mutch" on his head. She was rocking him when the press gang came in, but they never thought of looking in the cradle. The fishermen had all 'permants.' Each crew of a boat had to provide a man for the navy, which cost from £50 to £60. They then got their 'permant' or certificate that they were free from being pressed, and this they took to sea in a case, for fear that they should fall in with a cutter. If a crew were caught without having a 'permant' the whole crew, with the exception of the skipper and a man to take the boat ashore, were pressed. I remember a crew forgot to take their 'permant' to sea with them; they were overhauled by a cutter, and all but two men impressed. Boats went off after the cutter with the men's 'permant,' but failed to overtake her. The two men then went to the laird, James Gordon, and he used his influence to get the men free, which they did when they got to Portsmouth. It was from eight to ten days before they got home."

Sanitary arrangements have undergone a change. Each family used to have their "midden" close to the door. When empty the middens resembled round pits, six or eight feet in diameter, and as many in depth. Here water accumulated, and it was quite a trivial sight to see a tipsy native being fished out from one of these unsavoury baths; while on dark nights it was only the most cautious and those well acquainted with the geography of the district who escaped a fall or two. Let us narrate a story. In those old times it was customary for the parish minister to catechise old and young. On one occasion a small party assembled in the house of Coull, a merchant, who resided at Rathven. Among those present were Adam Downie, a lazy fisherman, and another man named 'Coull.' As the minister was late in turning up, liquor was sent for, and the party became pretty jolly. Adam, in one of his journeys, fell into an ash-pit or "midden," and was fished out in a woeful plight. He was being examined in the room, when news was brought that the minister was coming, and Adam was hastily forced into a "press" or cupboard. The catechising began, and the question were propounded by the clergyman - "How did Adam fall?" Coull stared at the interrogator, and then rising hastily up went to the press, opened the door, and cried to Adam to come out, as some "clashing" folk had told the minister all about it!

Each householder was wont to gather all the fish offal and shells into a pit, and when there was a sufficient heap collected a neighbouring farmer came and carted it away. Every farmer had two or three families from whom he obtained manure, as the contents of ash-pits and sea ware were the principal fertilisers up to 50 years ago. The middens have long since been filled up, the last of the race being the famous Nine O's of the Seatown. The invention of chemical manures gave the death-blow to those nauseous ornaments in a community.

Roads

The old highways are a subject of great interest to the student of antiquity. The most important road in this district was the highway, or "King's Get," as these roads were designated in the Scottish statutes of the 12th and 13th century. The road that runs along the Banffshire coast was constructed at the beginning of the present century. At that period John Loudon Macadam, a native of the town of Ayr, was endeavouring to introduce the system of road-making now known by his name. By 1815 his invention was adopted throughout Britain. Then the old highways were deserted for the new and better roads. The old turnpike road runs about the same distance from Buckie as does the more modern one. Part of it is to be seen as it crosses the ford at Hillocks, where an old rough milestone, with the number of miles from Banff on it, is still to be seen standing by the wayside. This road is of great antiquity, and winds over hills and dells. The present road is comparatively straight, and has been made as far as possible of a regular level. Having made the old roads the breadth required by law, rough boulders or rubble were thrown upon it by random, and roughly blinded by covering over with earth. These roads had to be repaired twice every year, and intimation was made in the Parish Kirk of Rathven on Sunday where the people were to meet for this purpose. Those who had a cart and horse had to give from four to six days' work in the year; and every labourer, cottar, tradesman, and fisherman had to bring a spade or pick. Those at a distance were exempted from this labour by the payment yearly of 6s ilk man, and 12s ilk horse. This was the origin of our yearly road and other county assessments. No adjoining proprietor could interfere with this road as it was public property, and if requiring to displace any part of it he had to do so at his own expense and to the satisfaction of the public. The roads next in importance to the King's highway were those that led to the kirk and mill. The present century opened with signs of great improvement in Buckie. The first ill-fated bridge over the Burn of Buckie, which was carried away by the floods of '29, was built. The most of the present roads were formed or improved, having been previously in such a state that it would have been impossible for traffic conveyances of anything resembling the modern make to have thundered their way through the town. Carts were then made entirely of wood, and very insignificant machines they were. The more common conveyances were termed horse creels. These creels were slung over the backs of the horses and were used in nearly all farming operations. The muck or midden creels, so called by Burns, were constructed on the principle that on drawing out a wooden pin the contents were emptied at once. A writer of that period says - "You will there yet behold simple John or Janet during the time of potato-setting or turnip sowing, ingeniously stationing the cadger horse in the furrow. Stooping beneath it to extract the pegs of both muck creels at once, frequently at this interesting moment by both hands not acting simultaneously, emptying the one creel on a sudden, this causes the other to descend with its load upon the unfortunate operator.

Mills

Since the introduction of steam and the great improvements in machinery of all kinds, the old mills have been allowed to go to decay. At one time there were as many as 24 water-power mills on the small brook of Tynet. Gollachy, Buckie, and Rathven burns were all well utilised in the manufacture of the various articles of commerce, such as linen, wool, cording, flax, meal, etc. The meal mills were considered most important to the needs of the community, and made the chief objects of many of the old statutes. They were supported by a law called thirlage, which came to an end in the reign of George III. Thirlage implied that certain lands within a given district were thirled to a particular mill, the people living thereon being compelled to grind their grain at the mill. The proprietor, or tackman, received multure or payment in a given quantity of grain. Those within the prescribed district were also bound to keep the mill in repair, and attend to the dam dykes, etc., and bring home the mill stones. Stories without end might be told of the deeds of the fairies, kelpies, brownies, and other supernatural beings at the old mills, which are generally situated in some den or hollow, where they can have the advantage of a good fall of water. A feeling of eeriness must have surrounded the whole scene, especially in the dark winter mornings, when the white form of the miller was to be seen moving about engaged in his various duties - the dusty air of the mill lighted up by the feeble flame of the fish-oil lamp as it flickered backwards and forwards in the draught, peopling the shady nooks with moving shadows. The splash of the water and the birr of the machinery might well excite the most dull imagination to flights of the wildest fancy, and shake the fortitude of the most sceptical doubter of the supernatural. The gist of most of the local legends is that the mysterious visitors to the mill did good or evil according to the character of the miller. If the miller was a kindly obliging fellow he was helped to manufacture the grain into meal, and would often enter the mill in the morning to find the day's work already done. He knew well enough to whose help he was indebted. In gratitude for the service done he would place clothes and food for his tiny helpers. Woe to the churl! All sorts of accidents happened to his mill. The dam would break out, the wheel would not go round, and often the whole establishment would be at cross purposes. The aim of these stories was to show how good actions were often rewarded, and evil suitably recompensed.

CHAPTER XIV

Castles

Buckie is not famous for the many illustrious personages who have paid it a visit. No houses are pointed out as having been the residence for a night or two of some king or queen. It was never made the recipient of a royal charter, nor was it ever the especial protege of a lord or a duke. To history it is unknown. Enzie men, however - and Enzie once implied a larger district than what it does now - have generally always been found fighting on the side of law and order. History more than once refers to the "Enzie men" being collected for the purpose of repressing some of the disorders that used frequently to break out. The Enzie, as it is now known, was once a very populous district, and many a sorrowful tale could be told about the numerous families who were deprived of their crofts and thrust forth upon the world. But if royalty did not reside often in the district, not a few castles have existed in the neighbourhood. On the west was Bog of Gight, or Bogen-Gight, now Gordon Castle. Shaw and others derive the name from Bog-no-Gaoith - that is, the "windy bog." Richard Franck, who made a journey through Scotland in 1658, describes "Bogageith, the marquess of Huntly's palace all built with stone facing the ocean; whose fair front - set prejudice aside - worthily deserves an Englishman's applause for her lofty and majestic rivers and turrets that storm the air, and seemingly make dints in the very clouds!"

To the east we have the Castle of Findochty which was likely a place of considerable note if we are to be guided by the ancient signification of the word Findochtie, which means "to find strength." The castle in all probability had its moat and drawbridge. Very little is left to show its former dimensions, the stones of which it was composed having been used for building purposes. It may be here noted that at Craighead Point, half way between Portessie and Findochty, about 200 yards to the right, may be found the Eglish Cave, the name of which suggests that at some early period it had been used as a church or place of worship. This idea is supported from the fact that a small haven lying between Strathline and Garbert Point, to the east of Craigenroan, has for a name Portcurrie, which signifies the port of the skin boats, and suggests that some of the early saints had arrived from Ireland at this place and met in the Cave of Eglish to conduct their services. A short distance off is the Law Hillock, a mound overlooking the sea, on the top of which there is an excellent spring. The Hillock had evidently been an old judgement hill, and an adjunct of the Castle of Findochty, which lies in S.S.E. direction. The outer terrace is 20 feet above the surrounding ground. About half a mile north of the moor at Findochty, and at a point lying between the crofts occupied by Mr Steinson and Mr John Davidson there is a place known by the name of the Gallow Hill, where it is most likely those who had to pay with their life the penalty of infringing whatever laws existed were executed after having received their sentences on the Law Hillock. Of recent date urns were found at this point containing ashes, but of course it cannot be certain whether these urns have any connection with the deeds which took place on the Gallow Hill.

Going a little further west we are told that two castles, the Green and Tronach, existed near the Harbour at Portknockie. Then we have the present Cullen House, and within the policies is the site of Davie's Castle. Further along the coast are the fine ruins of Findlater Castle "a miniature Gibraltar." Probably the castle was built in the 13th century. It is said to have fallen into the hands of the Scandinavians. There is a tradition that it was once a pirate stronghold. Near Portsoy is the Boyne Castle on Craig of Boyne, once the property of the Edmondstones, and then of the Ogilvies. It overlooks a deep ravine which served as a defence to the north-west; and on the south is the entrance by a raised causeway across the moat. The gateway is protected by two round towers, and the whole building consists of a rectangle defended by towers at the angles. In the latter part of the 16th century a hall 80 feet long was added. At Boyne Bay an older castle once stood upon the sea-shore, of which a few fragments remain.

Retracing our steps, and proceeding more inland, in the centre of the parish of Deskford, are the ruins of a tower of that name, an ancient castle said to have been built by the Sinclairs, the predecessors of the Ogilvies in the lordship of Deskford. In the same vicinity are the remains of the Castle of Skuth. In the "Gazetteer," published by Fullarton, is the following:- "In the institution at Banff is a curious antiquity consisting of a brazen swine's head, with a wooden tongue moved by springs. It was found about 25 years ago [i.e. 1818] in a mossy knoll at Leitchestown, near the farm of Inaltrie, which is supposed to mean the place of the altar, and where there are the remains of a very old and massive but anomalous structure, in one part of which there is a deep circular hole enclosed by a wall rising to a considerable height in the interior of the building. Close to it is a vault with a stair descending into it.

The Enzie used to abound with small lairds - at one time no less than about 20 existing in the parish of Rathven. At Leitchestown a tower was once in existence, and when his lairdship was at home the fact was notified by a flag floating in the breeze. On the Burn of Buckie, a little below the farm of Mill of Buckie, the site is pointed out of what is said to have been a rallying fort, to which the inhabitants of the district resorted in times of danger. The site would not have been an altogether unsuitable one, being surrounded on three sides by the Burn.

Robert Burns in the District

It has been said that there is no record of royalty having visited Buckie, but there is at least evidence that Scotia's darling bard, Robbie Burns, honoured Buckie with his presence, A few years before, Dr Johnson and Boswell passed Buckie on their westward journey during their famous tour in the Highlands. On the 25th August, 1787, Burns left Edinburgh, accompanied by Nicol, a master in the High School there, in a post-chaise, hired for the purpose. They journeyed through the heart of the Highlands, calling on and being hospitably received by many of the nobility residing in the line of the route taken by them. Among other letters of introduction Burns had one from Henry Mackenzie (author of "The Man of Feeling") to his relative, Sir James Grant, Castle Grant, which was as follows:-

Edinburgh, 24th Aug., 1787

My Dear Sir James, - This will be delivered by the Ayrshire bard, Mr Burns, of whom you have heard a great deal, and with whom Louis was acquainted here. He is also charged with a box for Miss Grant - I presume Miss Eliza - which came some time ago in the English stage coach, and was omitted to be sent by Mr M'Laren. It consists of such light materials as poets sometimes present ladies with. Mr Burns is accompanied in his northern tour by Mr Nicol, with whom I have not had the honour of being acquainted, but Louis, I presume, has a very feeling remembrance of him. You will find Burns not less uncommon in conversation than in his poetry - clever, intelligent, and observant, with remarkable acuteness and independence of mind - the last, indeed, to a degree that sometimes prejudices people against him, though he has, on the whole, met with amazing patronage and encouragement. Louis will show him the lions of Castle Grant, and as he is an enthusiast about the fortia focta patrum, let him not forget, as in the case of Lord Montboddo, to show him the large gun.

Penie still holds out, and is very well settled in Brown's Square, whither we removed immediately on the day you set out. We hope you have by this time finished your journey and found all well at home. Our love to you all. - Yours most affectionately,

Henry Mackenzie
Sir James Grant of Grant, Baronet,
Castle Grant.
Per favour of Mr Burns

After visiting Castle Grant, Burns proceeded down Strathspey, and then across the country to Fort George and Inverness. Having paid a visit to the Falls of Foyers he returned eastwards along the shores of the Moray Firth. On arriving at Fochabers Burns left his fellow-traveller at the village inn, and paid a visit to Gordon Castle, having become acquainted with the Duchess in Edinburgh the previous winter. The family were about to sit down to dinner, and Burns was invited to partake. Accepting the invitation he sat a short time at the table, and then arose and desired to withdraw, intimating that he had a companion waiting for him at the inn. It was proposed that a servant should go and bring Nicol to the castle, but Burns would not agree to this. He then himself proceeded to the inn, accompanied by a gentleman empowered to invite Nicol to the castle. When they arrived at the village they found Nicol in a great rage at Burns' seeming neglect, and ready to set off alone with the post-chaise. Entreaties were of no avail with the hot-headed schoolmaster, so that Burns had to forego the pleasure of a few days' stay at Gordon Castle. Burns and Nicol arrived the same night at Thorniebank, where they were most hospitably treated, music and dancing becoming the order of the hour. On the 9th of September Burns visited Buckie, and received a hearty welcome from some of the humble inhabitants. At that time, and at a later date, Buckie possessed a rich store of legends and tales. It was no uncommon feat to hear "The Gentle Shepherd" or "Tam o' Shanter" recited with all the rich melody of the native doric. Many of the inhabitants were able to recite ballads of 100 verses or more. A singer or a minister who used a paper or a book, no matter how well he acquitted himself, was unreasonably looked upon with feelings a little short of contempt for requiring aids to the memory. Burns had several old songs rehearsed to him during his short stay, one of which he remodelled as follows:-

A' the lads o' Thorniebank,
When they gae to the shore o' Bucky,
They'll step in and tak' a pint
Wi' Lady Onlie, honest Lucky!

Lady Onlie, honest Lucky,
Brews guid ale at shore o' Bucky;
I wish her sale for her guid ale,
The best on a' the shore o' Bucky

Her house sae bien, her curch sae clean,
I wat she is a dainty chucky;
And cheerlie blinks the ingle-gleed,
Of Lady Onlie, honest Lucky

Lady Onlie, etc

In "Rosetti's" edition of Burns' works we are told that "Bucky" refers to Buckhaven - a conclusion hastily arrived at, and certainly erroneous. Another old song of the same period, on another ale wife, was very popular. It began:-

Maggie Boungan on the Shore,

She's got painted on the door, etc

Lucky Onlie's house was situated near the site of Mr W. Thomson's house at Bridge End. It was a small thatched building, perhaps a little longer than the ordinary houses. Lady Onlie is described as having been "a clean, tidy little body," somewhat afraid of the sea, and wont to say to fishermen when she heard the wind blowing - "Do you hear that? You will not need to go to sea to-day. You had better get another 'chappin o' ale'." The night of her death is remembered yet by the fact that a schooner, blown from Helmsdale where she put ashore some passengers, sank in Spey Bay. The bodies of three or four of the crew were afterwards picked up and interred in Rathven Churchyard. Shortly after Lucky Onlie's death a sale of her effects took place. The auctioneer was one named Bennet, who caused a laugh at the expense of a Mrs Desson, to whom he remarked that a fine old-fashioned teapot which he was about to sell would be very suitable for a christening. What raised the laugh was the fact that Mrs Desson had no children. Burns' stay in Buckie was short, for on the 16th of September he was back in Edinburgh.

Buckie seems to have been a favourite visiting place of the old wandering minstrels and bards. Among others who came to Buckie was one Jock Milne of 'Livetglen, who always received good patronage and an interested audience. One of the rhymsters, referring to the Meal Riots in the north, when a detachment of soldiers had been sent to protect life and property, says:-

Of battles fought, and honours won,

Of bloodless deeds achieved and done

Where sabres gleamed and limpet knives,

'Twixt vet'rans stern and Buckie wives!

Alas! most of the poetical pieces that once delighted the inhabitants of Buckie in bye-gone days, have shared a similar fate to those who repeated them - their memory and their name are gone.

(The End.)